INTEGRATION NATION

Also by Susan E. Eaton

The Children in Room E4: American Education on Trial

*The Other Boston Busing Story: What's Won
and Lost Across the Boundary Line*

Dismantling Desegregation: The Quiet Reversal of
Brown v. Board of Education (with Gary Orfield)

INTEGRATION NATION

IMMIGRANTS, REFUGEES, AND AMERICA AT ITS BEST

SUSAN E. EATON

and

THE ONE NATION INDIVISIBLE WRITERS GROUP

THE NEW PRESS

NEW YORK
LONDON

Requests for permission to reproduce selections from this book should be mailed to: Permissions Department, The New Press, 120 Wall Street, 31st floor, New York, NY 10005.

Published in the United States by The New Press, New York, 2016
Distributed by Perseus Distribution

LIBRARY OF CONGRESS CATALOGING-IN-PUBLICATION DATA

Names: Eaton, Susan E.
Title: Integration nation : immigrants, refugees, and America at its best / Susan E Eaton
    and The One Nation Indivisible Writer's Group.
Description: New York : The New Press, 2016.
Identifiers: LCCN 2015025431| ISBN 9781620970959 (hardback) | ISBN
    9781620971420 (e-book)
Subjects: LCSH: United States—Emigration and immigration—Government policy. |
    Minorities—United States. | Race discrimination—United States. | United States—
    Ethnic relations. | Americanization. | BISAC: SOCIAL SCIENCE / Discrimination
    & Race Relations. | SOCIAL SCIENCE / Emigration & Immigration. |
    HISTORY / United States / 21st Century.
Classification: LCC JV6465 .E28 2016 | DDC 305.9/069120973—dc23 LC record
    available at http://lccn.loc.gov/2015025431

The New Press publishes books that promote and enrich public discussion and understanding of the issues vital to our democracy and to a more equitable world. These books are made possible by the enthusiasm of our readers; the support of a committed group of donors, large and small; the collaboration of our many partners in the independent media and the not-for-profit sector; booksellers, who often hand-sell New Press books; librarians; and above all by our authors.

www.thenewpress.com

Book design and composition by Bookbright Media
This book was set in Bembo and HapticPro

Printed in the United States of America

10 9 8 7 6 5 4 3 2 1

For my sons, Eli and Will, and their generation

Stories are the secret reservoirs of values. Change the stories individuals and nations live by and tell themselves and you change the individuals and nations.

—*Ben Okri*

CONTENTS

AUTHOR'S NOTE

This book emerged from the storytelling and organizing project One Nation Indivisible (www.onenationindivisible.org), which I founded and co-direct. Beginning in 2011, a group of experienced journalists and I set out across the country to write about the variety of efforts to assist immigrants in becoming full participants in the political, economic, educational, and social lives of their new communities. I wrote most but not all of the stories collected here. I am fortunate to have worked with extraordinary people who contributed to this book as members of the One Nation Indivisible Writers Group.

Helen Ubiñas, a newspaper columnist and reporter, wrote the story from Philadelphia. Tennessee-based freelance journalist Chris Echegaray and I collaborated on the story from Hazleton, Pennsylvania. Independent writer Meredith Carlson and I collaborated on the story from Montgomery County, Maryland. Chris Echegaray wrote the story from Dalton, Georgia. Freelance journalist and radio documentarian Barry Yeoman wrote the story from North Carolina. Journalist and former diplomat Omar Sacirbey and I collaborated on the story from Nebraska. I am grateful to Helen, Chris, Meredith, Barry, and Omar for their time, their attention to their craft, and their social concern. I hope we get to work together again one day.

INTEGRATION NATION

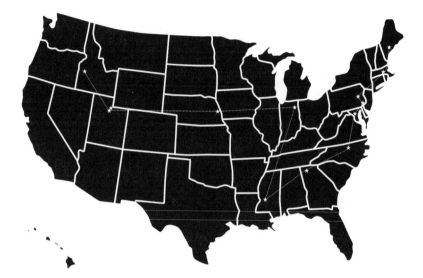

THE OTHER SIDE OF IMMIGRATION

In April 2010, Arizona's governor, Jan Brewer, signed a law requiring police to check the immigration status of anyone they suspected of being in the United States illegally. The law, SB 1070, imposed penalties for "sheltering" or employing undocumented people, and even for giving an undocumented person a car ride. The law inspired protests, boycotts, civil rights lawsuits, and some two dozen similar legislative proposals in other statehouses.

Several months after Brewer signed Arizona's law, Philadelphia mayor Michael Nutter hosted a festive public naturalization ceremony for new citizens. He threw a public party along the Benjamin Franklin Parkway. Beneath more than one hundred flags of nations that have or had a presence in the city, he helped swear in about twenty new citizens and raised the flags of nineteen more nations, including Botswana, Cambodia, and El Salvador.

"That was our response to the insanity out in Arizona," Nutter recalls. "That was our message to the immigrants who built this city and the ones who would help us revitalize it."

In 2010, Nutter's support for immigrants—he publicly urged them to move to Philadelphia—made him an outlier among elected officials. But several years later, he would sit squarely in the mainstream on immigration. Arizona and its legislative progeny dominated cable TV and blog chatter for years. But beyond that amplified nativist noise, many mayors, state legislators, and governors have joined civic leaders, educators, advocates, and millions of everyday citizens in a bipartisan "immigrant integration" movement aimed at assisting newcomers in becoming full, participating members in the civic, political, economic, and social lives of their American communities. A record 41.3 million immigrants—about 13 percent of the population—live in the United States, according to the U.S. Census. About one in four children in the United States has at least one parent who is an immigrant. Of the nation's 41.3 million immigrants, the census estimates that about 12 million are here without legal authorization.

The immigrant integration movement came into its own during an unlikely time, just as a flurry of Arizona copycat proposals promised to accelerate the deporting of undocumented people and to make routine life so difficult for immigrants and their families that they might decide to leave on their own. But only five of those laws passed—in Alabama, Georgia, Indiana, South Carolina, and Utah. And most of these have since been altered or watered down following federal court rulings and settlements with civil rights groups. Local officials in a handful of municipalities, including Farmer's Branch, Texas, Fremont, Nebraska, and Hazleton, Pennsylvania, also passed restrictive laws and ordinances. Those often imposed penalties for employing or even renting apartments to undocumented people. Federal courts struck down most of these local laws, too, usually after municipalities spent millions in legal fees. During this period, immigrants and their supporters expended so much energy and money fighting against restrictive legislation that they could hardly envision the kind of fairer, more sensible America we could fight for.

Around this time, I began working on a research project that brought me into deep conversation with resilient and hopeful people all around the country who were engaged in this sensible, constructive work. I spoke with classroom teachers, mayors, school board members, immigrants who had become effective advocates, to liberal, moderate and conservative lawmakers, soccer coaches, recreation center directors, bureaucrats, priests, rabbis, ministers, imams, tutors, young undocumented immigrants denied in-state tuition, small business owners who employed many immigrants, entrepreneurs who are immigrants, civil rights lawyers, scholars, and demographers. The more Fox News and MSNBC focused on Arizona and the like, the more I recalled the conversations I'd had with different sorts of people in many unlikely places. This included immigrants themselves and, too, U.S. citizens working alongside immigrants, developing programming, creating inclusive spaces, crafting humane and eminently intelligent policies, and establishing traditions that welcome, assist, and incorporate newcomers. Their stories didn't merely offer me comfort amid the xenophobia. They filled out a largely missing vision in the public conversation about building a better America.

Even as I began writing these stories, I knew that a heritage of people—quite often immigrants themselves—had been assisting new Americans and working to protect the civil rights of immigrants for generations. But by using the word "integration," the new movement's architects intentionally distinguished themselves from older efforts of assimilation, which historically have required a shedding of culture, language, and customs as part of the process of acceptance and success in mainstream America.

As Eva Millona, co-chair of the National Partnership of New Americans (NPNA), explained at a 2014 White House gathering on immigrant integration, assimilation "implicitly privileges" the values and interests of the "receiving community." In contrast, "integration," Millona said, "has come to mean valuing what diverse newcomers bring with them, as well as emphasizing what is needed to ensure their success and their potential contributions to the receiving community."

Big-city mayors were among the first who spoke publicly about the measurable benefits immigrants brought to their communities—not just Michael Nutter in Philadelphia but also mayors in Baltimore, Boise, Boston, Chicago, Cleveland, Dayton, and Jackson in recent years invited immigrants to settle in their cities and in some cases passed ordinances that forbid police from asking anyone about their immigration status. It is not surprising that mayors were among the first integration champions. Immigrant integration has traditionally been achieved at the local level. Unlike several other nations with a significant share of immigrants, our federal government has traditionally had a hands-off approach to immigration, with no official office or set of policies or dedicated funding streams that would ensure that immigrant newcomers settle successfully into their new communities. (The federal government does, however, provide some short-term assistance to communities that settle refugees.) Mayors, meanwhile, were seeing firsthand the role immigrants played in preventing or reversing population declines, in reinvigorating stagnant local economies, in contributing to rising entrepreneurial activity, and in adding less tangible cultural enrichments and vitality.

National organizations such as Welcoming America, with headquarters in Decatur, Georgia, and the National Partnership for New Americans, a coalition of state-level immigrant advocacy groups, grew into prominence and gained great influence and credibility during this period. Grassroots-driven, Welcoming America partners with affiliates in seventeen states, sparking dialogue, increasing knowledge about immigration, and fostering social relationships and cooperative action among foreign-born and U.S.-born people. The National Partnership for New Americans advocates for integration-related policies in states and at the federal level. Since 2007, NPNA has sponsored a crucial annual national immigrant integration conference bringing English-language teachers, clergy, local officials, and pro-immigrant governors and mayors together with top officials in the federal government, successfully uniting a community of people from a range of backgrounds, at various levels of government and practice, and with multiple vantage points. Attendance has increased steadily every year, and in 2014, more than a thousand people joined the conference in Los Angeles.

When I began learning about immigrant integration, in the early days of Arizona's SB 2010, I couldn't imagine that proposals for laws benefiting immigrants would ever get fair hearings in the political arena. But eighteen states now allow undocumented students to pay in-state tuition rates at public colleges and universities, with seven of these states adding these inclusive provisions and legislation after 2010. Ten states and the District of Columbia now permit people to obtain driver's licenses regardless of their immigration status, with eight states passing the laws in 2013. In 2014, after long consultation with the National Partnership for New Americans, President Barack Obama established the White House Task Force on New Americans. In 2015, the task force forwarded its reports and recommendations to the president. The task force called for more and more effective naturalization efforts, the promotion of civic engagement, and policies and practices that encourage and support immigrant entrepreneurs and protect the rights of immigrant workers.

What do integration ideals look like in practice? That's the most encouraging part of the immigrant integration story. In Philadelphia, city officials and nonprofits make it easier for immigrant entrepreneurs to do business, thrive in, and revitalize urban neighborhoods. After city leaders passed an anti-immigrant ordinance in Hazleton, Pennsylvania, immigrants and U.S.-born adults and children began participating in an array of programs at a new community center built to enable relationships and correct misunderstandings between groups. In Utah, educators bring together newly arrived Spanish-speaking students and U.S.-born English-speaking students who share classrooms and learn in both languages. Growing diversity in Nebraska inspired leaders of three religious faiths to share space for worship and social engagement. In Maine, adults created opportunities for young people of Somali descent to integrate on their own terms within the context of their family cultures and Muslim faith. In Georgia, doctors and nurses radically altered their traditional health care model and hired Latinas from the community to better care for underserved, undocumented immigrants. In demographically changing Montgomery County, Maryland, parents, teachers, and administrators systematically face their own racial and cultural biases as part of an ongoing effort toward building a cohesive school community. In Mississippi, African American elected leaders and labor activists work with undocumented Latinos, enhancing political power in a deeply conservative state. In Fort Wayne, Indiana, an abandoned theater has come back to life as a gathering place for refugees from Burma, Somalia, and Sudan, for Latino immigrants, and for U.S.-born residents, who share cultural celebrations and social events.

I chose to write about integration in practice not because discrimination against immigrants has ceased. Of course it has not. But the "Americans are angry about immigration" story is tired; it is covered over and over, rarely with satisfying resolution. Arizona's destructive policy is still an important story, but it is only one short chapter of a complex, ever-unfolding narrative about America and immigration in the twenty-first century. Exclusion and integration have long contended in our prevailing culture, in our politics, and to some degree in each of us. The people portrayed in this book teach us that we each have choices about how to think and act in the face of the rapid demographic change that is reshaping our country. The people we celebrate here deliberately chose inclusion over exclusion, open-heartedness over fear, and common sense over ineptitude. They move us forward. They represent America at its best. We would do well to follow their lead.

UTAH

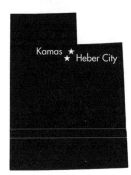

UTAH'S BILINGUAL BOON
A Red State Embraces Linguistic Diversity

When all the big changes came to Heber City, Utah, few people experienced them as keenly as Eric Campbell, the principal of a local elementary school, father of four boys, and pillar of his local church. Campbell and his wife, Melissa, had been one of the thousands of new families who had settled here over the past couple of decades, transforming this picturesque former farming community into a suburb.

The population had long been creeping up in Heber City. In 1990, just 4,300 people lived here. By 2012, more than 12,000 people called Heber City home. Hosting the 2002 Olympics had triggered a lot of growth in Utah. The international event expanded and improved infrastructure such as highways and drainage systems, and spurred development and tourism. After the Olympics, Park City, just fifteen minutes or so from Heber City, became an international tourist destination and outdoor playground for the superrich. Pre-Olympics, Heber City's newer families tended to have a lot in common with the old-timers. Most of them were white, politically conservative, and, like Heber City's founders, members of the Church of Jesus

Christ of Latter-day Saints, also known as Mormons. But post-Olympics, more and more of the newcomers stood out in the usual Heber City crowd.

They spoke Spanish, for one thing. They worshipped in Catholic churches, for another. A few years ago, Armando's Mercado opened up on North Main Street. A novelty at first, Armando's now enjoys a brisk business selling tortillas and homemade chorizo sausage to a mostly Mexican American clientele.

Eric and Melissa Campbell enthusiastically welcomed the cultural shift in Heber City, a place founded by English immigrant Mormons in the 1850s and named for the apostle Heber C. Kimball. Eric had learned Spanish during a two-year Mormon mission in Spain. Melissa had learned it during her mission in the Dominican Republic.

"Education is about expanding yourself," says Campbell, who is now director of elementary education for the Wasatch County School District in Heber City. "Different language, cultures, life experiences, and what have you. If you welcome this, if you are open, this will always enrich your life." Campbell's is certainly a forward-looking notion and a practical one for our globalizing society and his diversifying community. But amid Heber City's transformation, Campbell realized that the adjustments he would need to make as principal of Heber Valley Elementary School would entail more than open arms and elegant Spanish sentences. Most of the parents of his students had been drawn to Utah by low-wage service and hard-labor jobs generated by the Olympics. They fell squarely into the "working poor" category.

The vast majority of Heber City's Latino residents worked for low wages as maids, cashiers, cleaners, or cooks in booming Park City or in the other hotels and recreational businesses that had cropped up or expanded in the region. But few of the workers who kept Park City humming could afford the high rents there. Meanwhile, some of Park City's tourism riches trickled down to entrepreneurs in Heber City, where folks started or expanded their own outdoor recreation businesses, including cross-country skiing, snowmobiling, fly fishing, and hunting. These businesses needed workers to maintain trails, clean hotel rooms, and wait on tourists in restaurants. Some parents of Eric Campbell's students had two or even three of these kinds of jobs. Consequently, the poverty rate at Heber Valley Elementary kept going up. At the same time, grand wood-and-glass vacation homes with sweeping views quickly materialized high up in the hills on the way to Park City.

By 2013, about 55 percent of students at Heber Valley Elementary would come from families living below the federal poverty line, up from a not insubstantial 33 percent poverty rate in 2005. As is true in schools across the nation, a climbing poverty rate correlated with declining test scores. So, even as Campbell consistently stressed the "great assets" Latino students brought to the community, he could not ignore the fact that kids were clearly not meeting their potential. Some of the low scores were surely due to the fact that the increasing share of students still learning English had to take the state's mandated test in English before they had mastered the language. That aside, Campbell and many of his colleagues felt there must be a better way to reach students who were struggling. Campbell consulted with Linda Turner, the district's world language coordinator, who had grown up in the northern Mexican state of Chihuahua and had settled in Heber City after marrying an Utahan. Campbell was intrigued by the research Turner pointed him toward. Study after study demonstrated that English language learners tend to make more academic progress if they master a high level of literacy in their native language and work to retain that native language while they learn English as a second language. What's more, other research showed substantial long-term learning benefits for people who grow up speaking two languages. Campbell and Turner went to conferences to learn more. The method that seemed to show the best results for all students, Campbell told school board members and colleagues back in Heber City, brought together English-speaking students with Spanish-speaking students and taught all the kids in two languages.

As Campbell and Turner continued deliberating the merits of what's called "two-way immersion," Utah's lawmakers, fortuitously, were crafting a bill that would give start-up grants to local school leaders to begin foreign-language immersion programs.

Campbell and Turner jumped at the new opportunity, and soon after the bill became law in 2008, Heber Valley Elementary School enrolled ninety-six kindergarteners and first graders in a Spanish-English two-way immersion program. Since then, the program has expanded through fifth grade and enrolls about half of the school's five hundred students. Far more parents want to get into the program than can be accommodated. Encouraged by the success at Heber Valley Elementary, educators at two of the three other elementary schools in the community have adopted two-way bilingual programs, and plans are under way to bring a two-way bilingual program to the elementary school that doesn't yet have one.

Utah's inclusive educational response and embrace of bilingualism for all is unprecedented in the nation. In 2015, there are twenty-four two-way Spanish bilingual programs across Utah, and these are part of a larger language immersion effort in the state, which supports a hundred schools overall. The particular two-way immersion programs that bring together English speakers and native Spanish speakers were not invented in Utah and have existed in lots of places for decades. But no other state has expressed such unwavering political support and dedicated infrastructure to this form of bilingual education. Educators in search of ways to improve the achievement of English language learners, to enhance language learning, or to increase social cohesion in culturally diverse schools have flocked to Utah in recent years with the hope of replicating the state's progress.

"That this is happening in little red Utah really does still surprise some people," says Gregg Roberts, who helped shepherd the existing language programs into being as the world languages and dual-language immersion specialist at the Utah State Office of Education. The effusive Roberts has become something of an ambassador these days, speaking around the country to a growing audience of out-of-state educators and enthusiastically welcoming visitors to his home state. "I love what we are doing here. And I also have to say that I am really excited about our two-way Spanish programs," Roberts says. "I love talking about them. I love showing them off because so much of the talk in the education world about English language learners is all about, 'Oh, they need this. Oh, they are such a challenge' and blah, blah, blah. But two-way turns all that on its head. It says, 'Our Spanish speakers have talents and skills and let's build with that!' It says, 'We all need to adapt to the twenty-first century.' It's not this crazy idea anymore about *them* needing to adapt to *us*."

Like all good kindergarten teachers, Nuria Valero Martinez brings infectious exuberance, warmth, and patience to her classroom of five-year-olds at Heber Valley Elementary School. But Martinez, who came here from Spain, offers additional qualities, like language and culture, which are at a premium in Utah's public schools these days.

"Here, we have the days of the week," she tells her students in Spanish, pointing to the seven words written in colorful letters on the board. "Let's say the days of the week. . . ."

She and the children move on, reciting the months and then the numbers 1 to 31. "What day is today?" she asks in Spanish.

"Jueves!" the children shout, as if it being Thursday were the most exciting thing in the world.

Martinez continues, in Spanish: "And what month? What month is it now?"

Some of the children bounce up and down, clearly thrilled with themselves. "Septiembre!" the students chant.

Martinez beams at the children. "Muy bien!"

In a different class nearby, more kindergarteners review the names for shapes. "You guys are so smart!" the teacher says in English. The two dozen or so children scurry off to shared tables where they practice writing short words beginning with assigned letters. Things look much the same as they did in Martinez's classroom, but they sound very different here. After the two classes share recess, each group of students will trade classrooms, teachers, and the language of instruction. Later, Martinez and her English-speaking "partner teacher" will sit down to collaborate on lesson plans, strategies, and evaluations. It's right here in these classrooms where Heber City's new demographic reality is most visible. Heber Valley Elementary School's current principal, Jacki Burnham, estimates that about half of the children in her two-way immersion kindergarten classes are either immigrants themselves or children of immigrants, most of them with roots in Mexico. Overall, about 35 percent of Heber Valley Elementary's more than five hundred students are Latino, and well more than half of those are categorized as "English language learners." But it also is difficult to overlook the disproportionately high number of blond children here in Heber City, where many members of this still mainly Mormon community claim Swiss or German ancestry. Every summer, the neighboring town of Midway hosts a Swiss Days festival. Last year's celebration featured "Swiss tacos" in addition to the traditional "kraut dinner."

Rapid immigration increased the share of Latino residents in Utah from 9 percent in 2000 to 13 percent in 2012. In 1990, the state was 91 percent white, but demographers project that by 2030, the state will be just 72 percent white, as the share of the Latino population continues to grow. The share of African Americans here, by contrast, remains minuscule, at 1.3 percent. Multicolored signs and posters fill the hallway outside Heber Valley Elementary's two-way immersion classrooms. "Enter to grow in wisdom," reads one sign, with its Spanish translation below: "La puerta para crecer en sabiduria" (roughly "The door that will enable you to grow in wisdom"). Another, in Spanish: "Vengan a conocer mi lengua y mi cultura," which, translated to English, means roughly "Come and get to know my language and my culture."

"For my kids, it's been an incredible experience from an academic standpoint," says Joe Mellon who has two daughters and a son enrolled in two-way immersion at Heber Valley Elementary. "But there's so much to say as well about the other benefits. We have all these birthday parties going on all the time with kids from different cultures speaking in two languages with each other. That's the future right there, these kids working together and creating good things."

Under the Utah Dual Immersion law, passed in 2008, schools such as Heber Valley Elementary receive about $10,000 to start voluntary programs where students spend half the day learning in English and the other half in one of five languages: Spanish, Chinese, German, French, or Portuguese. In grades seven through nine, students in immersion programs take one class each year in their so-called target language, be it Spanish, German, Chinese, French, or Portuguese. They then take the Advanced Placement Language and Culture exam in ninth grade. (Usually students sit for such an exam in eleventh or twelfth grade.) In grades ten through twelve, students are offered upper-division university-level coursework through seven institutions across Utah. Immersion programs began in 2009, with 1,400 students in twenty-five schools. By the fall of 2013, about 20,000 students were enrolled in dual language programs in one hundred schools across the state. Immersion programs are never mandatory; in other words, a traditional monolingual educational program is always available for families. The Spanish two-way immersion programs found in Heber City are qualitatively different from the Chinese, German, French, and Portuguese programs precisely because of the growing presence and contributions of Spanish-speaking students.

"The immigration to our state is such a lucky gift," says Utah's

Spanish dual-immersion director, Ofelia Wade, who, as a Cuban immigrant, attended two-way immersion public schools in Miami. "This adds a richness and depth in the classroom that cannot be matched."

Utah's education officials at first worried whether $10,000 would be enough to inspire often already overwhelmed local principals to start new programs from scratch. As it turned out, local school boards lined up for the money. Each program uses two teachers, one who teaches in English and the other a native speaker of the target language. The state has hired teachers from France, Spain, Mexico, Argentina, and mainland China and brought them here on guest visas. The Spanish two-way immersion programs are spread throughout the state, including in affluent Park City, throughout Salt Lake City (where the concentration of Latino students is heaviest), in growing bedroom communities such as Heber City, and in rural communities. Overall, the state grants about $2 million each year for running the language programs. This equals about $100 for each student enrolled and pays for increased teacher training, costs associated with bringing over teachers from other nations, and curriculum development. State officials estimate that once the curriculum is written and paid for, the annual per-student cost will decline to $33. In New York City's private Avenues School, with a foreign-language immersion curriculum similar to Utah's, tuition is $40,000 a year.

Tax-dollar-supported two-way bilingual education might seem a radical solution for a place such as Heber City, where 72 percent of voters are registered Republicans. Some Heber City residents did have trouble taking to the idea of two-way bilingual education at first. "There was a for sale sign on my lawn and I didn't put it there," Eric Campbell jokes, recounting tense community meetings where people objected to the use of Spanish for instruction and expressed fear that monolingual teachers might be displaced, which never happened in Heber

City or in other communities with immersion programs. Others expressed a more generalized anxiety.

"You know, you had some people saying, 'We are going to fight against this because you are destroying our community,'" Campbell recalls. "But we just do not hear that anymore. I think we not only got past that, but we've all made incredible progress as a community. It's not going to happen overnight, but this program is exactly the type of effort we need to build those bridges between community members."

Researchers Virginia Collier and Wayne Thomas have studied two-way immersion programs for more than twenty years. In 2002, they published the most comprehensive analysis to date of the programs, examining data over eighteen years in twenty-three school districts across eighteen states for the U.S. Department of Education. Collier and Thomas concluded then that participation in two-way immersion programs was strongly associated with the narrowing of the achievement gap between English speakers and students still learning English. More recently, Collier and Thomas, under contract with the North Carolina Department of Education, evaluated two-way immersion programs in that state. After comparing two-way immersion schools to traditional schools with similar demographic makeups, they found that white students, Latino students, African American students, native English speakers, and native Spanish speakers all tended to make far more progress in two-way immersion schools (as measured by test scores), earn better attendance records, and receive far fewer referrals for behavior problems.

At the same time, the benefits of bilingualism have become increasingly clear. Cognitive neuroscientist Ellen Bialystock at Toronto's York University has conducted some of the most convincing research in this area. Her work finds that children exposed to stories in two languages tend to have advantages as they learn to read. More recently, Bialystock's studies suggest that bilingual adults are far less prone to cognitive decline than monolinguals, most likely because using two languages exercises the prefrontal cortex of the brain.

As the favorable research piles up, two-way bilingual advocates are quick to point out that two-way immersion's benefits likely extend far beyond teaching language and narrowing achievement gaps. Educators in Utah and elsewhere see two-way bilingual programs as particularly promising routes toward integration and community cohesion following a period of rapid demographic change. The state's Spanish dual-immersion director, Ofelia Wade, suggests this is because two-way immersion deliberately confers equal status and high value to the Spanish language and its speakers, unlike "English only" models that aim to teach students English quickly with no regard for preserving a child's native tongue. Two-way immersion, in contrast, views a student's home language and culture as, she says, "assets to build upon, preserve, and share."

"Learning a new language is not just the ability to speak a language and communicate. It is the ability to see everything more deeply, to see more, to hear different sounds that you have never heard before, to notice sights that you have never seen before and to hear voices that you have never heard before and to have perspectives that you would never have known existed," Wade says. "Learning a language is a strategy for breaking down barriers of all kinds. It is potentially transformative."

It is of course difficult to measure things like personal transformation. But educators in Heber City and in other communities agree that two-way immersion has helped spur more friendships between Latino and Anglo students, enhanced cultural sensitivity among educators and staff members, and created an avenue for white and Latino parents to get to know each other through their children. Jacki Burnham, principal of Heber Valley Elementary, notes that more Latino parents are volunteering in classrooms and "parents just seem to be more open and talkative" ever since the two-way program gained in popularity and Burnham hired a Spanish-speaking office secretary. Teachers at Heber Valley offer basic Spanish lessons to parents. Students from a local high school group, Latinos in Action, receive training and act as translators at Heber Valley's parent-teacher conferences and assist teachers in the classrooms.

"You know, occasionally you used to hear a student say things that were, well, unkind and reflected a kind of prejudice either about Spanish-speakers or other people who are not in the majority," Burnham recalls. "And we would sit down and have a conversation with that child. But ever since we've committed to our immersion program in this very open way, and we were able to have those community conversations about its value, you just don't hear it. . . . I think the children pick up on that fact that we value our Spanish speakers, that we see this cultural change as a positive."

Though still preliminary, the test results that so worried Eric Campbell years ago seem to be turning around. As one might expect from Spanish-speaking students required to take a proficiency exam in English before they've mastered the language, there's still a considerable difference in scores between English speakers and English language learners at Heber Valley. (For example, about 60 percent of English language learners were proficient in language arts in 2012 versus about 83 percent of English speakers.) But this gap has been shrinking over time. On math and language arts proficiency tests in 2012, about 20 percent more English language learners who had been enrolled in two-way immersion for three years at Heber Valley achieved proficient scores when compared with English language learners statewide not enrolled in two-way immersion. English-speaking students in two-way immersion programs tended to do better as a group on average than their counterparts in the school district and in the state overall. Encouraged by similar trends in other districts, Utah's State Department of Education is planning to apply for a federal grant that would allow them to more rigorously assess academic progress in all its language immersion programs, to assess students' proficiency in their second languages, and to explore parent and educator perceptions about whether two-way immersion programs have helped foster social cohesion, parent involvement, empathy, and cross-cultural relationships within schools.

Utah is often characterized as one of the nation's most conservative, "reddest" states. In reality, though, the state is a multidimensional place where pragmatism, a tendency toward kindness, and economic competitiveness blend to produce some curious policy outcomes. The 2008 law that created these programs is just one example.

The influence of the Mormon Church in politics and in the state more generally cannot be underestimated. About 62 percent of Utah's residents identified as Mormon in a 2012 survey, and the church's international headquarters is in Salt Lake City. In a 2010 statement related to immigration policy, the state's church officials noted that "the Savior taught that the meaning of 'neighbor' includes all of God's children, in all places at all times." Of the some 15 million Mormons worldwide, a little more than half live outside the United States. Beginning in their late teen years or early twenties, devout church members in the United States routinely take part in two-year proselytizing missions that often take them outside the United States. Educators here observe that missionaries typically return to Utah with a broadened worldview and well-developed empathy for people from a variety of cultural backgrounds. Recent surveys showed that about 70 percent of students at Brigham Young University, which is owned and operated by the Mormon Church, are bilingual. Former governor Jon Huntsman, who strongly supported and signed the 2008 dual immersion law, is a Mormon. So is Republican state senator Howard Stephenson, the legislation's principal architect and chief sponsor. Stephenson, from suburban Salt Lake City, is quick to mention his A+ rating from the National Rifle Association. And he is just as proud of being principal sponsor of the state's 2002 law that provides in-state college tuition rates for foreign-born students who are undocumented.

Restrictive immigration policies of the sort enacted in Arizona in 2010 have fallen out of favor in most states ever since Latino voters helped propel President Barack Obama to a second term in 2012. But well before this shift, Utah's lawmakers had parted ways with other red states when it came to immigration policy. Less than a decade after passing the in-state tuition law, Utah, in 2010, became one of just a few other states at that time to allow undocumented immigrants to get driver's licenses. (Since then, lawmakers in several other states, including California, Maryland, and Illinois, have passed similar measures.) Around the time that Arizona's lawmakers passed its notoriously restrictive immigration law, a group in Utah that included police officers, state officials, elected leaders, business leaders, and religious leaders crafted the Utah Compact. Based on what signatories call "Utah values," the compact outlines principles to guide discourse and policy making about immigration in the state. Heralding a "free-market philosophy" and expressing opposition for policies that "separate families," the compact states: "Immigrants are integrated into communities across Utah. We must adopt a humane approach to this reality, reflecting our unique culture, history, and spirit of inclusion. The way we treat immigrants will say more about us as a free society and less about our immigrant neighbors. Utah should always be a place that welcomes people of goodwill."

Integration has not always been a hallmark of the Mormon Church. From 1852 until 1978, the church barred its black members from becoming priests, from getting married in the temple, and from other church rituals. Church leaders for generations advanced theories about black inferiority to justify the church's discrimination, although such theories were publicly rejected by scores of younger and more progressive Mormons. In December 2013, the Mormon Church, acknowledging intentions to further expand across the globe, released an official statement disavowing "theories advanced in the past." The statement stressed that church leaders now "unequivocally condemn all racism, past and present, in any form."

Many of Utah's political observers acknowledge that while prevailing Mormon morality is always a variable in political outcomes, dual immersion was sold to lawmakers and to the public mainly as an economic development measure. It is true that Howard Stephenson, the dual-immersion law's chief sponsor and cheerleader, tends to speak first and foremost in economic terms. Stephenson says he was originally inspired to craft the law after meeting bilingual schoolchildren in China and worrying that our batch of mainly monolingual American kids would never measure up in a "global marketplace." A bilingual workforce, Stephenson says, will attract business and revenue to Utah. It will "equip our schoolchildren to compete in an international economy." But even after ticking off this series of sensible-sounding bullet points about "prosperity" and "competitive advantage," Stephenson just keeps on talking about the "gift" and "the opportunity for personal transformation" provided by the "presence of our Latino brothers and sisters." He even tears up a little.

"I mean, for John to be sitting next to Pablo and be learning in Spanish, it's just such a great experience for kids and it really bonds communities together. It builds bridges," Stephenson says. "We are just so lucky. And so the English-speaking families see the Spanish-speaking students as a benefit, as community members with just as much value and rights and wonderful attributes, rather than just looking at them and thinking something like, 'Oh, those are illegals.'"

To the rare critics of dual language or of immigrant integration measures in general, Stephenson responds: "Look, our state has changed. The little rural communities, little towns are all changing. If you celebrate that, if you give our young people a place to blossom and grow and to really integrate, if you create the opportunity for all of us to integrate and to each come over to the other's perspective a little bit, how can that not be good for everyone?"

It was around 2002 when teachers in the rural town of Kamas (population 1,270), about a twenty-minute drive east from Park City, began to realize they had better get certified to teach English language learners. Louise Willoughby, the spirited homegrown principal at South Summit Elementary School, encouraged her staff to do just that. Then in 2013, Willoughby and Barry Walker, the district's superintendent, decided to take what Walker termed "an even bigger and better step further." They applied for one of the state's dual-immersion grants so they could start a two-way bilingual program, which is now in its second year. So many Spanish-speaking English-speaking parents wanted to sign their children up that Willoughby had to turn several families away.

"I think it was just good that we chose to do this. I think it communicates to the Hispanic members of our community, 'We are happy that you are here.' Kamas was traditionally a [Mormon] community. Everyone was Mormon. Growing up, I think I knew one family who was not Mormon," Walker says. "The Hispanic people who came in are Catholic. And so there wasn't that mixing of cultures because the central social experience here is through the [Mormon Church]. And so, this, I think this program, is a start of bringing folks together." Kamas started to become more diverse in much the same way Heber City did.

Just before the 2002 Olympics, developers had constructed a new highway that cut the drive from Kamas to Park City from an hour to just twenty minutes. Suddenly, this isolated rural village began to evolve as an affordable bedroom community for people who worked in Park City and even in Salt Lake City, about a forty-minute drive west.

First-grade two-way immersion teacher Letecia Heredia came to Kamas from the city of Cuernavaca, in central Mexico. "I was not sure what to expect, but I really love it here," she says. "You know that children and families have left Mexico and come to the United States, and so to come here and see that people want that culture, that they want to learn, and that I can help the Spanish-speaking students keep their language and I can share with American students is really great for me."

In Heredia's classroom, which features a cozy reading corner decorated with Mexican blankets and flags, the children gather their coats and line up to head home for the day. In Spanish, Ofelia Wade, who is visiting for the afternoon, asks several of the students: "What languages do you speak?"

Every child, Latino or Anglo, responds in Spanish. Their answers: "I speak English and I am learning Spanish," or "I speak Spanish and I am learning English," or simply "English and Spanish."

One of the students tells her that he and his family are from Jalisco, Mexico. He then asks another visitor if she speaks Spanish. The woman tells him, in Spanish, that she is still learning Spanish. The boy squints at her and grins.

"You need help," he tells her in Spanish. "A lot of people want to learn Spanish. It is one of my languages. If you want, I can teach you."

—PHILADELPHIA, PA—

Philadelphia ★

BEYOND BROTHERLY LOVE

Philadelphia's Bet on Attracting and Retaining Immigrants Pays Off

On a warm spring afternoon, Herman Nyamunga makes his way down a dense eight-block section of Woodland Avenue in Southwest Philadelphia. He moves quickly, ducking in and out of stores with the ready smile, quick wit, and outstretched hand that people along this busy, slightly scruffy business corridor have come to depend on.

On paper, Nyamunga, who has an MBA and a background in the import-export business, is a "small-business development coordinator" for the Welcoming Center for New Pennsylvanians, a nonprofit employment and referral resource for the region's growing immigrant community. But in the moment-to-moment reality of Southwest Philly, this Kenyan immigrant is more of a mentor, a trusted adviser, and, today, much welcomed company.

"I've come to visit," he announces playfully in one store, the mischievous glint in his eyes getting brighter. On one block, Bain's Halaal Market, owned by immigrants from Ivory Coast who moved to Philadelphia about ten years ago from

New York City, sits across from Smiles Linens, owned by Bruce Zeiger, of German descent. Nearby, Nina's Grocery—a one-stop shop stocking everything from African foods to clothes and soaps—faces Butcher Block Meats, one of what locals call a "legacy" family business, where generations of Americans of Italian descent work side by side. And so it goes, up and down the avenue. Longtime business owners who have weathered multiple, sometimes seismic economic and demographic changes make a living alongside immigrant entrepreneurs helping to revitalize one of Southwest Philadelphia's key commercial corridors.

"Parts of Woodland Avenue for a long time were just vacant space, and now there are all kinds of businesses opening. This is like the UN," Nyamunga says delightedly, glancing down the street. He bounds into another store.

Anchored by the historic Episcopal Church of St. James at 68th Street and the University of the Sciences in Philadelphia at 45th Street, Woodland Avenue is this neighborhood's three-mile-long commercial and residential spine. As longtime business owners proudly point out both in conversation and on their business association websites, Woodland Avenue is rich in history if not always in dollars. It was part of America's first north–south highway. In the early to mid-nineteenth century it was a popular destination for family shopping and gathering. Much of that early shine wore off as the region's manufacturing declined and then accompanying urban challenges, including unemployment, growing poverty, and middle-class flight, hastened the downward spiral. But increasingly over the past decade or so, new neighborhood stores, fueled in large part by immigration, are breathing life into the area.

Inside Nina's Grocery, Nyamunga and owner Nina Williams talk business. There's not enough, declares Williams, who is originally from Sierra Leone. Has she considered going in with other business owners on bulk items, such as rice? Nyamunga suggests. She hasn't, but tells Nyamunga she'll consider it. A few doors down, store owner Fanta Diaby and Nyamunga exchange a few quips before he asks Diaby if she's applied for the city's storefront improvement program, which Nyamunga had mentioned during a previous visit. It's a program open to both immigrant and American-born business owners; the Butcher Block's owners recently got help buying new refrigerated display cases.

"Did you fill out the paperwork?" Nyamunga asks Diaby.

Diaby, a reserved woman wearing a multicolored dress and matching orange head scarf, smiles sheepishly as she shakes her head. "No, I was waiting for you to help me."

"You need a better sign," he gently chides her. "How else will people know you are here?"

"You know we are here," she jokes.

When Diaby emigrated from Ivory Coast to New York City, there were days she wouldn't utter a word outside her home, if she even ventured that far. Often, she said, she felt alone, desperate to communicate and share about her life in Africa. Standing by a wall of ornate dresses and shoes imported from Dubai, Diaby recalled her early frustrations in Philadelphia.

"I could not tell them who I was," she says, watching cars pass outside her store's front window. "I could not tell them what I did in my country." Diaby had been a grocer in Ivory Coast, just as she is again, in her new country.

Back in New York, when Diaby wasn't working at a grueling job as a nurse's aide, she would lock herself in her apartment and watch television. She laughs at the memory. "The television was my teacher. All the time, I watched television."

By the time Diaby moved to Philadelphia in 2001, she had picked up enough English from sitcoms and police dramas to be able to open the business on her own.

"It was very difficult," she recalls. "Everything we did, everything you see, we did everything on our own."

But then Nyamunga showed up on the avenue, and she and her husband, who runs the business with her, quickly found an invaluable friend in "the man with the answers." To gain that trust, Nyamunga knows it takes building a rapport and a relationship with both U.S.-born and immigrant business owners, who can be suspicious of each other and suspicious, too, of strangers bearing gifts. "He comes to say hello, to help us . . . to bother us about the sign," she jokes while looking over her shoulder to see if Nyamunga is listening. He isn't. He is busy leaving a message for a colleague at the Philadelphia Department of Commerce's Office of Business Services, which helps immigrant businesses gain access to city services and programs.

The Welcoming Center, where Nyamunga works, is not a city agency, though the city's commerce department is one of the Welcoming Center's major funders. The Welcoming Center's business outreach workers often collaborate with city officials as part of the city's lauded Global Philadelphia program. Since its inception in 2003, the Welcoming Center, founded by Irish immigrant Anne O'Callaghan, has helped more than ten thousand immigrants from 140 countries through its programs and outreach. They provide assistance with finding jobs, learning English, getting access to legal services, and small business support.

Amanda Bergson-Shilcock is the Welcoming Center's encyclopedic director of outreach and program evaluation. "We were really born out of the very practical recognition that there was a need that wasn't being met," she says. "None of the immigration organizations in the area were focused on employment and none of the workforce organizations in the Philadelphia area were focused on immigrants, and yet what our founder discovered was that immigrants kept coming in the door looking for jobs."

Not only were immigrants coming for jobs, but they were also looking for help in starting their own businesses. A study by the New York–based Fiscal Policy Institute found that between 1990 and 2010, immigrant businesses accounted for 30 percent of the nation's growth in small businesses. (Small businesses are defined as those with fewer than a hundred employees.) But beyond the economic mission of the center, Bergson-Shilcock is quick to point out that there are equally important perceptual and philosophical missions that drive the Welcoming Center's work.

"First of all, we don't see immigrants as needy victims. We see immigrants as talented assets, and that's the big difference. Many of our clients have survived tremendous trauma. But people are more than the worst thing that has ever happened to them. Our approach—even our location, here in the middle of Center City—is about saying that we take them and their goals seriously. It's about showing trust and respect in our clients by saying, 'You've survived enormous amounts of dislocation and sometimes hardship in your country. You've made your way to a new country. You've sometimes brought your children and others with you. But we trust that if we give you a road map, you're going to make your way.'"

Around the same time that the Welcoming Center opened its doors, the city launched an initiative called Global Philadelphia, designed to ensure that city services were accessible to people who did not speak English. The initiative, which is run out of the city's Office of the Managing Director, was part of a long, evolving response to Executive Order 13166, signed in 2000 by President Bill Clinton. The order required federal agencies to improve services to people with limited English proficiency. It required the same from agencies that received federal funding. Two subsequent local mandates reinforced the order, at least in theory.

"Back in early 2000, the way that the city was responding to its immigrant population in terms of services was just piecemeal," says David Torres, the assistant managing director who oversees Global Philadelphia. "You may have been provided services or you may have been turned away."

In 2008, city officials discovered that several city departments either had never drafted or had shelved their language access plans. That same year Mayor Michael Nutter signed an executive order mandating "all city departments, agencies, boards, and commissions to develop, assess and improve language access plans regardless of whether they received federal funding or were overseen by the managing director." Services have consistently improved, Torres says. But it's still a work in progress.

"One of the biggest challenges is that staff oftentimes view the tools themselves as a hindrance to getting their job done—calling an interpreter takes more time," Torres adds. "So changing attitudes, changing hearts is a huge challenge. It's also about attitudes toward immigrants, and when you have an organization that is as old as ours, you have city staff who have been here a really long time, you have folks that have been here twenty-plus years, and they oftentimes forget what it means to be an immigrant in Philadelphia."

Philadelphia's deputy mayor and managing director, Richard Negrin, says the diverse cultural backgrounds of people in the city's administration seem to help. Negrin's family, for example, fled Cuba in the 1960s and settled in New Jersey.

"When we talk about major policy situations, and I am in the room, and others in this administration who are sensitive to those issues are in the room, it matters," he says. "In a lot of ways, Philadelphia is going back to its roots. People once came here primarily for religious freedom. Now, it is economic opportunity that is good for them and, frankly, us."

Subsequently, city employees developed two important practices that seem to be working well: in-person and over-the-phone translation, and "language access cards." The cards—available in more than a dozen languages, including Cambodian, Bengali, Korean, and Arabic—allow a person who speaks a language other than English to come into a city office, pick up the appropriate card, and hand it to a city employee. The card informs the employee of what language that person speaks and what services they need. Cards can also be downloaded from the city's website and instruct the user how to get access to a variety of city services. It also helps that, for the most part, financially strapped city departments don't have to foot the bill for the services. Citywide, Torres says, Philadelphia spends about $500,000 on language access services yearly, with the majority covered by taxpayer dollars (from the general fund) and federal grants.

Philadelphia's Commerce Department has long been a leader in language access efforts. Two years ago, the department brought on six multilingual AmeriCorps VISTA workers to connect with immigrant business owners across the city. The VISTA workers teach small business owners about the role of various government offices and introduce them to the government employees with whom they will need to work in the process of opening and operating a commercial enterprise in the city. They also walk owners through the complicated licensing process and help them navigate the multiple city departments with which small business owners need to interact.

"We are sensitive to the immigrants of the city and that experience, but it's just as much about sensitivity as it is about survival of the city," says Shinjoo Cho, the technical assistance and outreach manager for the city's commerce department. "They are inevitably tied." Cho, a native of South Korea, began her career with the city as a business development liaison. Now she is in charge of recruiting, training, and deploying the AmeriCorps VISTA workers.

Before taking his current job at a North Philadelphia nonprofit, recent college graduate Manuel Martin was a VISTA volunteer working with Cho. Canvassing another of Philadelphia's business corridors in the 9th Street Italian Market, the boyish-looking Martin talks about the challenge of building relationships with immigrants who may come from countries where they are, with good reason, fearful of government officials.

"It has to be about building a relationship first," he says, echoing what the Welcoming Center's Nyamunga had said weeks earlier. "They don't always know what to make of you. You can see the look in their eyes, like, 'OK, what's the catch?'"

Philadelphia's elected leaders have, in recent years, followed the proven logic that helping foster vibrant, prosperous immigrant communities will benefit everyone. In the past five years, the city's Global Philadelphia program has been strengthened by strong community connections and by Mayor Michael Nutter and his administration. "We know from research and history that, certainly for many big cities, growth comes from an influx of immigrants," says Mayor Nutter, who has been in office since 2008. "That's been New York's experience, that's been Boston's experience, Chicago and a number of other cities. Immigration has been an incredible part of Philadelphia's past, but it is also a great part of our future."

Therefore, he says, the city's approach has to be deliberate, swift, and purposely opposite those of municipalities and counties—from Prince William County, Virginia, to Farmer's Branch, Texas, to Hazleton, Pennsylvania—whose efforts to reduce their immigrant populations have led to economically disastrous results, deep fractures in the community, or both. Shortly after Arizona passed its notorious anti-immigration law, Mayor Nutter hosted a naturalization ceremony for new citizens on the Benjamin Franklin Parkway, lined with more than a hundred flags from different countries.

"That was our response to the insanity out in Arizona," he says. "That was our message to the immigrants who built this city and the ones who would help us revitalize it."

The city's approach, Nutter stresses, is basic. "The first way to demonstrate that you're an immigrant-friendly city is for the government to be immigrant friendly," he says. In this sense, Nutter is borrowing talking points from his former City Council colleague James Kenney. Back in 2000, Kenney had been a lone and controversial voice when he suggested that immigrants could reverse the city's population slide. He even called for hearings on ways that the city could increase immigration.

"There's a moral component to this," Nutter says. "But there is absolutely an economic component to it, too, and that's the future of this city. Part of our survival is going to be about our continued ability to diversify and transform, and that means embracing change. You either grow or you die. You move forward or somebody's moving ahead of you. Our survival depends on our diversity of people and economics."

Kenney and Nutter seem to be on to something. The Metropolitan Policy Program at the Brookings Institution reports that among its peer regions, metropolitan Philadelphia has the largest and fastest-growing immigrant population. The region's 500,000 immigrants make up 9 percent of its population. Brookings researchers also found that between 2000 and 2006, greater Philadelphia's immigrant population grew by 113,000, nearly as many immigrants as arrived in the 1990s. Brookings researchers then broke down Philadelphia's population, revealing a diverse mix of immigrants and refugees from Asia (39 percent), Latin America and the Caribbean (28 percent), Europe (23 percent), and Africa (8 percent), with the ten largest source countries being India, Mexico, China, Vietnam, Korea, Italy, Ukraine, Philippines, Jamaica, and Germany.

Few numbers were quite as significant to Philadelphia as the results of the 2010 U.S. Census, which not only helped Philly keep its ranking as the fifth-largest city in the country but also reversed a fifty-year population decline with growth that in large part was due to increased immigration. City officials were ecstatic.

"Today, I am proud to be the first mayor since Mayor Samuel in 1950 to announce an increase in Philadelphia's population," Nutter said in announcing the census results. "It is no coincidence that the strategic investments we made have attracted new individuals to our dynamic, growing communities. We have newcomers arriving in Philadelphia from all over the region, the nation, and the world. It is my great pleasure and honor to say we are back. Philadelphia is growing. Philadelphia is rising."

In spite of the optimistic press conferences, though, the city's demographic change has not come without conflict.

In 2005, the owner of a landmark South Philadelphia cheese-steak stand in the historic 9th Street Italian Market garnered national attention when he put up signs telling customers: "This is America. when ordering speak english." At the time, Joey Vento—who told reporters that his Sicilian-immigrant grandparents had struggled to learn English—said he was concerned about immigration reform and an increasing number of people in the area who could not order in English.

After investigating, the Philadelphia Commission on Human Relations found that Vento was not in violation of the city's Fair Practices Ordinance. Vento died in 2011, but his sign remains. And in 2010, the Philadelphia School District signed a two-and-a-half-year settlement with the U.S. Justice Department to address violence against immigrant students at South Philadelphia High School. The Justice Department investigation had been triggered by twenty-six assaults on Asian immigrant students in 2009. After the settlement, more than fifty Asian students organized a weeklong boycott to protest what they felt was an inadequate response to what they described as years of harassment and violence. Their efforts brought attention to tensions throughout the Philadelphia public schools and prompted the creation of a district-wide Task Force on Racial and Cultural Harmony.

"You can talk to a lot of people," the Welcoming Center's Bergson-Shilcock says, "and they'll tell you that the [settlement] should have covered more than just one school."

Federal, state, and local lawmakers will likely continue to argue about immigration in the coming years. But meanwhile, cultural negotiations, ethnic change and adaptation, and day-to-day life will go on at South Philadelphia's 9th Street Italian Market, which looks just like many of the local neighborhood business corridors across this city. Iconic Italian businesses such as Ralph's Italian Restaurant sit next to Vietnamese poultry markets, which are surrounded by Mexican restaurants and shops. Latin music spills into the traffic-choked street. In the past ten years, an estimated twenty thousand Mexican immigrants have settled in South Philly. One enterprising Vietnamese hair salon advertises with signs in English, Spanish, and a variety of Asian languages.

At the Tortilleria San Roman, a small corner shop where a family makes and sells Mexican tortillas, Mario Rivera works the cash register. Manuel Martin, the VISTA worker, has dropped by to introduce himself. Stout and serious, Rivera begins telling Martin the story of his family business and the challenges he's faced. The family started the business with a small card table right out front, Rivera tells Martin, motioning out the window. After years of saving the profits from $1 and $2 bags of tortilla chips, they finally had enough cash to buy the small store they were both standing in.

But owning a store, Rivera explains, didn't make opening or running a business any easier. Traditional banks are often out of reach for immigrant business owners. City inspectors were unsure of how to inspect the hulking piece of equipment in the middle of the store that Rivera uses to make tortilla chips. Rivera shakes his head at the memory of the baffled city inspectors and smiles. Rivera mostly nods politely while Martin explains why he's there and then starts to talk about the ways the city could assist Rivera. It's clear that Rivera is intrigued. The two shake hands, and Rivera tells Martin to come back anytime.

"Running a business is hard work," Rivera says. "But at least now we have our proper store, our proper place."

MISSISSIPPI

Hinds County

SAME NEW STRUGGLE
Building a Better Southern Strategy in a Changing Mississippi

To find the new Mississippi, drive north from its capital, Jackson, and in a few miles exit off the interstate and enter a maze of suburban cul-de-sacs. Pass the seemingly limitless numbers of brand-new and still-emerging identical brick single-family houses budding from ground where crops used to grow. Slosh through copper-colored mud. Walk under tarps and into the home in progress. There Julio Gomez balances expertly on red metal stilts. He grips the edges of a section of drywall and positions it over a wood frame. His screw gun buzzes the thirty-pound slab into place. Below Pablo Cruz—who, like Gomez, left his native Veracruz, Mexico, and hiked through Arizona desert for this job—slices through another piece of drywall. He hoists the unwieldy rectangle to Cruz, who clomps over the concrete floor to cover the next spot.

In the home-to-be next door, Miguel Garcia spreads white glop over the minute vertical spaces between drywall sections the men hung a week earlier. After the mixture dries, Garcia will sand it and, in time, paint over it. Everything will appear seamless. Potential buyers will see no space between slabs, no screws, and no sanded sections. All that work, suddenly invisible.

Just about anyone buying one of the newly constructed homes off Mississippi's main highways, or a new dining room table for it built in one of the state's several surviving furniture factories, or a chicken slaughtered and cleaned in one of the poultry processing plants here, purchases what is often still hidden: Latino labor. But even after well more than a decade of steady immigration to cities, suburbs, and rural townships throughout the Deep South, Latino immigrants often remain underappreciated, ignored, or worse. Since the late 2000s, a virus of draconian anti-immigrant legislative proposals has spread through the southeastern United States, finding eager hosts in South Carolina, Georgia, and Alabama. (In June 2012 a U.S. Supreme Court decision made some provisions of the harshest laws unconstitutional.) But annually it meets a surprising death upon reaching Mississippi, getting killed by a multiracial political coalition nurtured by diverse membership and led largely by African American legislators who years ago decided to take on the immigrants' cause as their own. The alliance between African American lawmakers and civil rights activists, white progressives, immigrants, and their supporters persists as a hopeful model for other states where African American elected leaders have increasingly taken leading roles in opposing anti-immigrant proposals.

"The Black Caucus knows its history—many of our members lived that civil rights history—and we vowed to never sit still when human beings are being treated as less than human," says James Evans, who began his sixth term in Mississippi's state legislature in January 2015. In the late 1950s and early 1960s Evans's father had worked side by side with Medgar Evers, the civil rights activist and NAACP field secretary who was assassinated by a white supremacist in Jackson in 1963. Evers was mourned nationally and immortalized in poetry, books, and films, and his spirit haunts this state and Jackson in particular, where his modest house has been transformed into a museum. "You can still see the bullet holes in that house," says Marcia Weaver, a former Jackson city councilor and local historian who welcomes tourists to her small bed-and-breakfast in the city. "That struggle lives in our air here."

Civil rights still commands moral authority in what might be considered its epicenter, Mississippi, just as it does in its neighboring southern states. Alabama's white state legislators may have overlooked this, just as they failed to appreciate the profound interdependence between immigrants and the native-born. Alabama legislators who had supported recent anti-immigrant legislation seemed unprepared for the anger directed at them not merely from national human rights groups but also from local watermelon and catfish farmers and building contractors who had lost their workforce and suffered diminished profits. Perhaps more damning, though, is that supporters of this legislation are now cast as new villains in a familiar southern struggle.

"One of my concerns is that this bill opened up some old wounds that it didn't need to open," Alabama state senator Gerald Dial, who in 2012 said he regretted voting for the law, told *Bloomberg Businessweek*. (All except one of Dial's fellow Republican legislators voted for the Alabama law, known as HB 56.) "All of that stuff from the Fifties and Sixties—Alabama is not like that anymore." Alabama's law represents by far the most drastic of all the recent legislation aimed at immigrants without documents. As passed, it requires educators to verify a student's immigration status before the child can register for public school. It even makes it a crime to give an immigrant without "papers" a ride in a car.

Texas congresswoman Sheila Jackson Lee, who is African American, recently said the law in Alabama had created a "civil rights crisis." In December 2014, civil rights activists and immigration advocates gathered in Birmingham to revisit Alabama's segregationist history, to decry its contemporary immigration legislation, and to develop ways to join forces to counteract those impulses.

Historians and scholars, too, draw attention to the stark similarities between the "states' rights" argument that shored up segregationists in the South in the 1960s and justifications for immigration legislation today. "Alabama now risks going down in history for its intolerance toward undocumented immigrants and Latinos as well as African Americans," writes University of California, Davis, law professor Kevin Johnson in the *Stanford Law Review*. Shortly after the law passed in Alabama, Latino immigrants began to flee the state. According to immigration lawyers and immigrants in Mississippi, many Alabama escapees sought work and sanctuary in Mississippi.

"It is not an easy life here either," says Mississippi Immigrant Rights Alliance (MIRA) community organizer Juan Carlos Cook, an Ivy League–educated, thirtysomething Mississippi native. (Cook has since moved on from MIRA.) In addition to working as a community organizer, Cook for a while took over his Mexican friend's small construction business after his friend was deported. "Everything is relative. People are afraid to go out of their houses here, too, and for good reason. But you have people literally running from Alabama. I hope they can find safety here. There seems maybe a little more hope in Mississippi, at least for now."

As a child, Cook had endured the sparsely attended Spanish Mass at the Cathedral of St. Peter the Apostle Catholic Church in downtown Jackson. His mother, Martha Cook, had grown up in the northern Mexican city of Juárez. She immigrated to Mississippi in 1979 to marry Cook's father, a Mississippi native who traveled regularly to Mexico on business. Martha Cook still attends the Spanish Mass every Sunday. These days, though, she has to arrive early to get a good seat in crowded pews. She no longer lacks volunteers to organize the traditional Mexican Our Lady of Guadalupe procession each winter either.

"It's become a whole new world here," Martha Cook says.

"I love to see it happening. I know not everyone in Mississippi loves these changes. I have lived here for many years, so yes, yes, I know that."

The Latino population is growing faster in the South than it is in any other region of the United States. Between 2000 and 2011, Latinos accounted for about 45 percent of the region's population growth. This is far more than the growth attributed to whites (22 percent) and African Americans (19 percent). Among southern states, Mississippi still has one of the smallest immigrant populations, with an estimated 2 percent of the population foreign-born and about 3 percent Latino, according to the U.S. Census. (Comparably, about 8 percent of North Carolina's population is Latino. About 9 percent of Georgia's is.) Immigrant advocates in Mississippi insist those numbers vastly undercount the immigrant population. Even assuming the numbers are accurate, the Latino population in Mississippi from 2000 to 2013 has increased 117 percent, making it one of the states with the fastest-growing Latino populations.

Long before Latinos made much of a showing in the census numbers or at the Cathedral of St. Peter in downtown Jackson, a white labor organizer named Bill Chandler began laying the groundwork for a multiracial, multiethnic coalition in support of immigrants, both those who are legally present and those who are not. In the late 1990s, Chandler had been working as a union organizer throughout the South. He had met Latinos, mostly from southern Mexico, who had come for work in the state's burgeoning chicken processing industry. Soon after the legislature permitted casino gambling throughout the state in the early 1990s, the corporate owners hired cheap Latino "guest" labor, first to build gigantic hotels and later, after their visas had expired, to work under contract cleaning the hotels and casinos. Given Mississippi's famously scarce resources, Chandler feared that tensions between Latinos and African Americans over jobs would develop and quickly be exploited by cynical politicians. Chandler, who had grown up in racially diverse Los Angeles and worked alongside Cesar Chavez for the United Farm Workers, figured the best way to dissipate that tension was to bring both groups together in a strong alliance as organized workers so that "everyone would benefit" from fair wages and safe working conditions.

In 2000, Chandler was meeting with a social worker in her office about reports of Latino workers who had confronted their bosses about working conditions on the Gulf Coast and who were now being threatened with deportation. During the conversation, a Methodist minister named Mary Stewart called in tears looking for Chandler, who just happened to be in the social worker's office. She explained that educators in Laurel, about ninety miles southeast of Jackson in the Pine Belt, were refusing to enroll the children of Latino poultry workers. The school administrators insisted that the children needed Social Security numbers to be enrolled.

Stewart told Chandler of the overwhelming number of complaints she had received from desperate and frightened parents. Chandler knew that in 1982, the U.S. Supreme Court in *Plyer v. Doe* ruled that children cannot be denied an education because of their immigration status. Chandler set out to address the immediate constitutional violation in Laurel. (With Chandler's urging, African American state senator and former teacher Alice Harden would introduce a bill, passed in 2002 and based on *Plyer v. Doe*, that established a process for education officials to register and enroll children who are undocumented immigrants.) Chandler was moved to help these particular immigrant families get their kids into school. But it also inspired him to start an organization devoted specifically to protecting immigrant rights.

"If you look at the issues that immigrants are concerned about—jobs, work conditions, access to a good public education—they are not that far from the same issues that African Americans have been talking about," Chandler, who is now in his early seventies, says. "So it was an idea that began developing very rapidly." Chandler and his growing collection of allies calculated that with the continuing growth of the Latino community in Mississippi, an active alliance with African Americans represented "an opportunity for serious political change" that would benefit people of color and working-class white people. As more Latinos became integrated into their new communities, and perhaps earned green cards and later citizenship, Chandler and his African American allies saw that "voting patterns would also shift, bringing a possible transformation to this state over the next ten or twenty years."

One of the first decisions made by Chandler and the small staff at the newly developed Mississippi Immigrant Rights Alliance was that they would never ask a white ally to introduce legislation that was explicitly designed to benefit immigrants. MIRA always turned to well-respected black leaders with a strong standing in the civil rights community, so that immigrant residents would immediately see African Americans as their allies and begin to build familiarity and trust between the two groups. This included Rep. James Evans, a union organizer and ordained Presbyterian minister; Rep. Willie Bailey, a well-known defense attorney in the city of Greenville; Sen. Alice Harden, of Jackson, the former public school teacher who also had been a union leader; and Rep. Edward Blackmon Jr., a defense attorney in suburban Canton, where increasing numbers of Latinos were coming for work in the town's chicken processing plants. In deeply red Mississippi, the alliance nearly got a bill passed in 2001 that would have issued driver's licenses to undocumented people.

African American civil rights advocates sit on MIRA's board. Those board members, along with African American legislators, regularly march, speak, and recruit people to join in MIRA's rallies. African American legislators even take to the airwaves to counteract what Rep. Evans calls "hate radio" and to dispel negative myths about immigrants. Over time, the widely read Spanish-language newspaper *La Noticia* began featuring prominently placed photos of African Americans standing up for immigrant rights at rallies and demonstrations. Patricia Ice, an African American MIRA staff attorney, who is also married to Chandler, writes a weekly column in *La Noticia* on a variety of legal issues such as racial profiling and ensuring care of minor children in the case of deportation. Ice also writes a column for the *Jackson Advocate*, the paper that serves the city's African American community.

"We made sure Patricia's picture was right there at the top of her [*Noticia*] column, too," Chandler says. "It's important for immigrants to see this, to see African Americans taking on these causes, to understand who their true friends are."

African American legislators, including Evans, Blackmon, and Bailey, won appointments to important committee chairmanships in part because they had supported a white Democrat, Rep. Billy McCoy, in his hotly contested 2008 campaign to become Speaker of the House. McCoy, a worm farmer from a small town on the Tennessee border, had faced a tough challenge against a conservative Democrat, Jeff Smith, who has since become a Republican. The more moderate McCoy evolved as a strong supporter of immigrant rights, along with other measures, such as adequate public education funding, environmental protection, and provision of adequate benefits for the poor, all of which had traditionally been supported by members of the Black Caucus.

Alongside this still blooming multiracial alliance, another Mississippi clings to its symbols of oppression and its tradition of resistance to civil rights. Mississippi is the only state that still incorporates elements of the Confederate "Stars and Bars" in the official state flag flying prominently in front of the statehouse and other government buildings. (In a 2001 referendum, 65 percent of voters said they wanted to keep the flag. The predominantly black Delta region, not surprisingly, wanted it gone.) Marble statues of Confederate soldiers stand outside courthouses here. Jackson's water supply comes from the Ross

Barnett Reservoir, named for the staunch segregationist governor and member of the White Citizens' Council, a white supremacist group.

About 37 percent of Mississippi's residents are African American, the largest share of the total population of any state. In 2010, about 45 percent of the state's African American residents lived in poverty. In the legislature, the membership of the Black Caucus was never large enough to pass bills that did not also have significant support from white legislators. But members could, through their committee chairmanships and with Speaker Billy McCoy's support, kill what Rep. Evans characterizes as "the really, really bad bills that called out for it, the most morally repugnant, the bottom of the barrel: The immigration bills."

In 2011, Republican lawmakers had introduced thirty-three bills that aimed to either deport more immigrants, make life and work nearly impossible for them, or merely exclude them symbolically. One bill would have restricted an immigrant's ability to rent an apartment, even though federal courts have ruled similar bans unconstitutional. Another bill would have denied people without documents access to public benefits, even though this is already prohibited under federal law. Still another would have mandated "English only" in conducting government business. By spring, all the bills had died. This even included the harshest, SB 2179, an Arizona copycat, which had previously passed both houses and which even the most hopeful observers had assumed would become law. Legislative maneuvering by two Black Caucus members who had the support of McCoy and of another powerful white Democrat, Rep. Bobby Moak, managed to kill the bill. Similar scenarios had played out in previous years, as anti-immigrant bills died in committee.

Later in 2011, Tea Party favorite Phil Bryant, a Republican who had long been an outspoken critic of "illegal immigration," was elected governor on a strong anti–illegal-immigrant platform. And for the first time since Reconstruction, Democrats lost control of the Mississippi House to Republicans, who already controlled the Senate. In 2012, Speaker Bill McCoy retired and Republicans appointed new chairs to legislative committees.

"Within thirty days, we're going to see a radical restructuring of state government like we've never seen before," Mississippi NAACP president Derrick Johnson told the audience at the state's Black Leadership Summit shortly after the November 2011 election. "Within thirty days, it's going to look like 1962."

In that well-remembered year, 1962, white segregationists rioted in Oxford, Mississippi, over the admission of James Meredith, an African American military veteran, to the University of Mississippi. Mississippi's governor at the time, Ross Barnett, had attempted to bar Meredith's admission. Two people were killed in the riots and at least seventy-five people were injured. President John F. Kennedy called in federal troops to quell the rioting. Two years later, U.S. lawmakers passed the Civil Rights Act and then, in 1965, the Voting Rights Act.

As expected, in 2012, Mississippi Republicans, with Governor Bryant's strong support, did indeed propose another measure aimed at undocumented immigrants. This bill would have required police to check the immigration status of any person arrested. It also included sanctions for employers who hired undocumented people. When first proposed, it even included a provision (later removed) requiring school officials to tally the number of students who are undocumented immigrants and to stop utility companies from providing electricity or water to people who are known to be undocumented immigrants. That year, though, strong opposition to the bill came not only from African American legislators, MIRA's membership, and other civil rights groups but also from several business groups, including the Mississippi Poultry Association, and from law enforcement officials who expressed concern that the law would damage trust between police and members of the immigrant community. The state's Catholic bishops and other faith leaders also spoke out against the measure. The bill passed the House but died in a Senate Judiciary Committee chaired by a Democrat who refused to put the measure up for a vote. In 2013, another bill that would have strengthened the system that employers use to confirm that a worker is not an undocumented immigrant also died in committee.

Two years later, in 2014, Mississippi Republicans again introduced a bill that would have criminally punished undocumented residents who were working in the state. That same year, though, Democrats introduced two bills of their own. One would have granted in-state tuition rates to college students who are undocumented, and another would have allowed undocumented immigrants access to compensation in the event of a workplace injury. During a hearing on the tuition bill, in a committee room on the first floor of the statehouse, MIRA members draped a traditional Mexican blanket over the statue of former two-term Mississippi governor and U.S. senator Theodore Bilbo, an ardent segregationist who had been a member of the Ku Klux Klan. Draping the blanket, MIRA's Patricia Ice explained, is a "way of kicking [Bilbo] out of our meetings." The statue of Bilbo, who died in 1947, had been in the rotunda until former governor William Winter had ordered it removed from that prominent location. None of the immigration bills made it to the floor for a full vote. In late 2014, MIRA members held meetings to discuss how to strengthen future in-state tuition bills. The following year, legislators reintroduced yet another bill that would provide undocumented students in-state tuition rates.

MIRA, its allies, and immigrants are up against more than just unsympathetic state legislators. In some sense, say Chandler, Ice, and other immigration attorneys in the area, any legislation that might pass in the coming years would give official sanction to some local police officers who already try to enforce federal immigration law, and may embolden other officials to do the same. Experienced immigration lawyers in the Jackson area say their clients are frequently victims of roadblocks set up by county sheriffs and local law enforcement, who are ostensibly checking for insurance, seat belt use, and valid driver's licenses and registrations. The website roadblock.org contains numerous reports of locations in the state where police and sheriff deputies stop drivers and ask them for identification. Attorneys and undocumented immigrants themselves say that local police and county sheriffs routinely stop Latinos for no cause or for what seem like invented reasons—for not wearing a seat belt, for example, or seeming to drive erratically. These stops don't always end in arrests, but they do contribute to a culture of intimidation and profound mistrust.

In the town of Pearl, just east of Jackson, the local city council in 2010 unanimously passed an ordinance that restricted the number of people who could live in a rented apartment or mobile home. The ordinance required that a sleeping space be at least 100 square feet for two people and an entire apartment housing two people be at least 220 square feet. MIRA and other human rights organizations framed the ordinance as a thinly veiled effort to criminalize immigrants who had in recent years moved into apartment complexes in Pearl, which is predominantly white and working-class.

On the Catholic holiday Ash Wednesday in 2011, local Immigration and Customs Enforcement (ICE) agents raided homes and other locations in the towns of Pearl, Canton, Raymond and Carthage, ostensibly rooting out immigrants who had been convicted of crimes, though priests and others reported that many law-abiding people were rounded up and were so terrified that they fled. Around the same time that year, as part of a weekend-long raid outside Jackson, ICE agents raided the Colonial Terrace apartment complex in Pearl, where many immigrant families live. Immigrants reported numerous abuses that occurred that evening to MIRA officials, the press, and local attorneys. A man reported that an ICE officer had held a gun on him while he lay on the ground, handcuffed. When the man's young son cried and complained, the man reported, the ICE agent had briefly turned the gun on the boy. A woman claimed that when ICE officers knocked on the door, sometimes they claimed they were selling Avon cosmetics; other times, the residents recalled, the officers told residents they were delivering pizza.

A small but meaningful counterweight to the ICE raids and the local ordinance in Pearl came from the city of Jackson, whose majority-black city council in 2010 passed an anti-racial-profiling ordinance that prohibits police from asking people about their immigration status. The legislation, which passed on an 8-to-1 vote, is modeled after a similar ordinance in Detroit. Patricia Ice of MIRA wrote the legislation. City councilor Chokwe Lumumba, a prominent African American civil rights lawyer who would later be elected mayor of Jackson, introduced it. (Lumumba died in 2014 at age sixty-six after only eight months in office.)

"To the Latinos who don't feel welcome elsewhere, I think they should come to Jackson," Lumumba said in a 2012 interview. "It's good for us politically; it's good for our economy now and into the future."

Rep. James Evans is proud that Mississippi has mapped out and nurtures "a new kind of Southern strategy"—one that fosters alliances between people who have similar values but come from different racial and ethnic backgrounds. Evans's purposeful choice of the word "new" reframes the "old" Southern strategy pioneered by Richard Nixon, who exploited white southern racism to win over Democrats disgruntled and disaffected after desegregation and passage of the Civil Rights Act of 1964 and the Voting Rights Act of 1965.

"This is a fight against the kind of venom that black people in Mississippi understand on that heart level," Evans says, tapping his heart. "But this is hearts and minds working together. Walking together is how we all win, now and further down this long road."

As they continue to strategize in order to stave off anti-immigrant legislation today, Bill Chandler and Patricia Ice realize that they must look toward the future, too. They believe that, even if they lose their legislative battle and Mississippi goes the way of Alabama, Georgia, and South Carolina, they have not only morality and the civil rights narrative but also the numbers on their side. This is one reason that, in addition to advocacy and organizing, Ice convenes frequent naturalization workshops around the state for legal immigrants hoping to become citizens. She helps them fill out the voluminous paperwork required for citizenship applications, study for citizenship exams, and, if necessary, bring their English up to the level they need to pass the oral part of the test. Each year, more and more people join MIRA's marches. In early 2015, MIRA brought immigrants and their supporters from the Gulf Coast to join in a Civic Engagement Day, when they met with state legislators urging them to fight against restrictive immigration measures and to support the bill calling for in-state tuition for undocumented students.

Over the years, Chandler, Ice, and MIRA's community organizers and student interns have spent a lot of time in and around Jackson meeting with immigrants. Not long after the raids of 2011, organizers had visited a dusty trailer park in Canton, Mississippi, where they had spoken with dozens of Latino immigrants about the harsh immigration-related proposals before the legislature. Most of the immigrants who rent the dilapidated trailers here work in the chicken processing plants that have become a staple industry in Mississippi. Isela Gonzalez hangs and cleans chickens in a Peco plant next to the trailer park. She listened to MIRA staff members and decided to attend the rally.

Waking up on the day of the rally, Gonzalez, who was pregnant at the time, remembers feeling "tired and sad," as she often did those days. Her common-law husband and father of her unborn child had recently been deported, she said, after a sheriff's deputy stopped him while he was walking back from work and asked him for "papers" that he did not have.

"I became happy when I got to the march," she says, cradling her newborn son in her arms. "I saw that we are not alone. There are people with us." Gonzalez says she joined "a lot of Mexicans and Guatemalans and white people" that day, adding, "I saw many more black people who seemed like important people, the bosses, that day."

The alliance between African Americans and Latinos in Mississippi upends the narrative that casts African Americans and Latinos as adversaries in a zero-sum game. As journalist David Bacon has documented in his book *Illegal People*, many African Americans in Mississippi have indeed seen themselves displaced by employers who have hired more easily exploitable Latino workers. But as Bacon also points out, and as MIRA's Chandler and Ice take pains to bring to light, the villains here are the less visible forces undermining economic security for all low-wage workers. Research bears this out. After conducting a large statistical analysis, Yale University economist Gerald Jaynes testified to Congress in 2007 that he and his colleagues found only very modest effects upon African Americans' wages resulting from immigration. Jaynes stresses that the decline of manufacturing, weakened unions, a computerized information economy, and educational inequality are far larger threats to African Americans' economic stability than immigration ever was.

"Look, everyone needs to put food on the table. Everyone wants to walk down the street without getting harassed," Chandler says in MIRA's Jackson office. Outside his door, Latino immigrants sit waiting for a workshop on the naturalization process to start. "We need to respect the different histories here between groups. But the folks in that waiting room and African Americans looking for a living wage? They are engaged in the same struggle. And it is not with each other."

BOSTON, MA

Boston ★

WHAT IS FOUND
IN TRANSLATION?

For Bilingual Interpreters, a Path
Out of Poverty; for Medical Patients,
an Amplified Voice

A woman stands and thrusts her right fist in the air. She pokes her thumb out from between her index and middle finger.

In her native country, Russia, she explains, this gesture means, "'You will get nothing more from me. I am finished talking.' . . . It can also mean 'Go away.' But it is stronger than 'Go away.' It's not a friendly thing to do. So I'm going to stop doing it now."

Laughter erupts in this classroom of about thirty women from all over the world—women who speak many different languages and share a common aspiration to climb out of poverty by doing good and increasingly necessary work.

"That's so interesting!" another student exclaims. "Because in Brazil, that same sign with the thumb and fist? That means good luck. Or it's like saying, 'Everything is going to be great for you.'"

A woman from Colombia adds, "In my country, to say that you are tired of talking, you do this." She makes a cutting motion with her hand across her throat. "That's saying, 'This conversation is over.'"

Student Krystie Bellabe, who spent much of her childhood in Haiti before attending high school in the United States, adds: "See, in the U.S. dragging your hand across your throat? I think you use that when telling someone else to be quiet. Am I right?" Her fellow students murmur agreement.

"Can we get back to the fist and the thumb?" one student asks. "I think it's obscene in some cultures."

A student from China confirms that yes, in some Asian cultures the gesture would be considered "not very nice at all."

The class instructor, Inna Persits-Gimelberg, originally from what is now Belarus, in the former Soviet Union, reminds students: "You cannot know the meaning of every gesture everywhere because these things evolve. Your interpreting practice will always be a work in progress. The point is that you need to interpret nonverbal communication. . . . The patient deserves the opportunity to express themselves in their full humanity."

The students' origins span the globe. Because of this, some of the women in this donated classroom at Boston's Beth Israel Deaconess Medical Center would look at a thumb poking through a fist and find offense or feel rebuffed. Others would see hopefulness and well-wishes. But as Persits-Gimelberg strings together the words "opportunity," "expression," and "humanity," this spectacularly diverse classroom becomes a sea of nodding heads. It seems that everyone here understands precisely what she means.

More than 25 million people in the United States—a little less than 9 percent of the population—are not proficient in English. This is an increase of 80 percent since 1990. In Massachusetts, the share of people with limited proficiency in English slightly exceeds the national average. Federal law and laws in every state guarantee medical patients with limited proficiency in English the right to a free competent interpreter and to translated "vital" medical documents, such as consent forms.

This particular class, organized and sponsored by a small local nonprofit called Found in Translation (FIT), is different from typical medical interpreter courses, which are proliferating as linguistic diversity and the concomitant need for interpreters increases across the nation. For one thing, it is offered free of charge to bilingual women who earn very low incomes. And unlike other courses that require only fluency in two languages and money up front for tuition, the Found in Translation course is highly selective, with 234 applications this year for fewer than three dozen spaces. Found in Translation is the brainchild of twentysomething Maria Vertkin, an immigrant from Russia via Israel. Soon after graduating from nearby Regis College, Vertkin became a social worker and youth advocate for a variety of agencies and nonprofits in and around Boston. She couldn't help but notice the high levels of homelessness, poverty, and attendant personal crises among the immigrant women and their families she got to know. But that was not all she saw.

"I think we tend to think in terms of what immigrants need, as opposed to what they have. And one of the great assets a lot of women I met had were language skills and very strong, very adept cultural navigation skills," Vertkin says. "Then you have a huge medical community that I figured had to need bilingual talent. It just seemed logical to match these things up."

Vertkin researched the job projections for the medical interpretation field and found her hunch about growth and need to be correct. According the U.S. Bureau of Labor Statistics, the field is projected to grow by 42 percent over the next decade. Vertkin also figured out that the typical medical interpreter salary—about $45,000 a year or $30 to $40 an hour—would increase a typical Massachusetts homeless family's income by about 530 percent.

"At first I thought, 'Great! I have solved the problem.' But when I tried to get some of the women I worked with to sign up for a course, I quickly saw if you don't have $1,000 just lying around, you cannot take this course. Or if you have kids and you have no one to watch them and you can't afford a babysitter, you cannot take this course. If you don't have a car or if you don't live near public transportation, you cannot take this course. So my goal became getting rid of all those irrelevant things."

And so, along with standard introductions and icebreaking exercises on the first day of class, Found in Translation staff members also match students with carpools. During class, volunteers offer a free on-site play group for the students' children. Throughout the year, FIT staff members offer workshops on résumé writing, job interview skills, how to use social media, how to manage a bank account, how to create a budget, and how to prepare taxes. Networking events bring potential employers and students together. A local photographer takes professional portraits for the online LinkedIn profiles that Found in Translation staff members help students to set up. An alumni group provides ongoing job search help as graduates enter the workforce.

"We create an environment so that women in the class really support each other," Vertkin says. "Someone has lost a loved one or has a child care crisis? We figure out how to assist the student and get them whatever help they need to stay on the path and complete the course."

To attract a diverse pool of candidates, Vertkin and her staff post fliers at churches, mosques, cultural dance classes, agencies that serve people with low incomes, and ethnic restaurants. From the 2014 applicant pool, Vertkin, volunteers, and staff interviewed eighty candidates, looking for women who demonstrated motivation, a strong grasp of English, and the ability for self-reflection. Then they narrowed that group to a class of thirty-four students. In 2014, the represented native languages include, but are not limited to, Spanish, Portuguese, Chinese, Hindi, Amharic, Arabic, Dutch, Somali, Russian, Haitian Creole, French, and the principal Senegalese language, Wolof, also spoken in Mauritania and Gambia.

All of Found in Translation's students qualify as having low incomes, and the majority of the women have been homeless for significant portions of their lives. Some of the students in the 2014 class have no high school degree, and others have a general equivalency diploma (GED). A few are highly educated, with advanced degrees. Several had been professionals—doctors, nurses, education officials—in their home countries but have operated cash registers or cared for the elderly or for other people's children in the United States. Nearly all the students in the current class are immigrants, though a few are children of immigrants. In order to qualify for the program, a candidate must be a woman; either homeless, recently homeless, and/or low-income; eligible for work in the United States; and fluent in English and at least one other language. Found in Translation, with a staff of four, survives on small foundation grants and holds two fund-raisers each year—a sunset bike ride and a multicultural dinner and dance.

"In recent years, as we have seen the demographics of our region change, you've seen an increased appreciation for the art of medical interpreting," says Shari Gold-Gomez, director of interpreter services at Beth Israel Deaconess Medical Center in Boston. "This program is so inventive and the people involved with it are so committed and bring such diversity and such incredible talent to the field. Once I have openings, I am hoping to have the opportunity to hire some of the graduates."

The twelve-week, sixty-hour certification program has so far granted certifications to three classes of women in as many years and boasts a 96 percent graduation rate. The course, which is twenty hours longer than standard classes of its type, requires women to memorize dozens of medical terms—"cataracts," "anemia," and "blood sugar," to name a few. The women learn about homeopathic remedies used in various cultures and the intricate ethics governing the interpreting field.

In a recent class, students learn that they must never help pick up a patient who falls or reposition an uncomfortable patient who can't do it herself. Persits-Gimelberg, the instructor, explains that "all these matters must be left to a medical professional," adding, "there may be instances where the patient feels comfortable with you, because of the language commonality, the cultural connection, and asks you to help. But you cannot help in that way."

A few students scrunch up their noses. Others look back and forth at each other with wide eyes.

Perhaps sensing the discomfort in the room, Krystie Bellabe speaks up.

"See, in a lot of our cultures, that probably seems strange," she says. "I mean, just as a human being, you know, the human kindness culture, or however you want to call it, you see a person fall and you rush to pick them up. But the way I think of it is that we are learning another culture, and that is the medical culture."

"That is a perfect way of stating it," Persits-Gimelberg says. "It may not feel natural to just stand there. But with all of your experiences negotiating cultures, I have faith that you will learn not just the rules but the complex medical culture very quickly."

Escape is the dominant theme in stories that Found in Translation's students tell about their pasts—escape from violence, sadness, abuse, oppression, deprivation, and discrimination. In talking about their present and about the future they envision, the women do express eagerness to escape again, this time from poverty. But they also voice a desire to settle down into meaningful work.

The path that led Fatou Sidibe to the Found in Translation class started nearly four thousand miles away on Africa's far western coast, in her home country, Senegal. In 2000, Sidibe left her family and community to join her husband, who had come to the United States from Senegal a few years before. When the marriage did not work out, Sidibe left a lot behind, including a roof over her head. For a couple of years, she and her school-age daughter lived in shelters while Sidibe worked at a variety of jobs. One of her favorites was at a taqueria in Cambridge.

"It seems funny, right? An African woman making tacos? Well, I loved it," Sidibe says. "Most of them were from Mexico, and maybe it seems we would have little in common. That was not true. They are like family to me now." In addition to English and her native Wolof—which is the most widely spoken language in Senegal—Sidibe speaks Senegal's official language, French, and Spanish, which she studied back home in school.

Soon after Sidibe scraped together enough money to get a small apartment for her and her daughter, she saw a flyer for the Found in Translation course in Harvard Square. At the time, she was working, raising her daughter as a single parent, and taking classes through Harvard's Extension School in the hope of eventually earning a bachelor's degree in government and then looking for work in the international human rights field.

"The minute I saw [the flyer], I thought, 'What a wonderful thing!' I would like to be contributing to the world in that way,'" she remembers. "I could immediately see myself doing this kind of work. Just the thought of it felt right from the very beginning."

In addition to the responsibilities of a working parent and a part-time student, Sidibe also volunteers several mornings a week at Boston Medical Center's food pantry. Each month the food pantry, the first of its type in the nation, serves more than 7,500 families who cannot afford healthy food. Patients at Boston Medical Center receive prescriptions to the pantry from their medical providers, who specify the health-related reason—diabetes, say, or hypertension—for prescribing particular foods.

In this helping role, Sidibe is unfailingly positive, finding reasons to celebrate even the less loved of the root vegetables. She rolls a cart full of healthful food—whole-wheat bread, tomatoes, brussels sprouts, dried beans, and a softball-size rutabaga—to the door, where a client, a small-statured, middle-aged woman, waits.

"What is that?" the woman asks, pointing to the rutabaga, also known as a Swedish turnip.

"The rutabaga is a really great thing. I use it like a potato," Sidibe tells the woman. "You can really do so much with it. It's going to absorb all the flavors in a stew, or you can mash it up. And it is so filling."

The client smiles. "Okay, then. I'll give it a try and report back to you."

The woman tells Sidibe that she is from Cameroon.

"Oh! I am your neighbor, sort of," Sidibe tells her. "I am from Senegal. And now I am your neighbor in Boston!"

Sidibe volunteers at the hospital food pantry, she says, for the same reason she was drawn to interpreting. "I cannot have my life be just about me, me, and me and just what I want," she says. "I have had so many opportunities in this country through [Found in Translation]. So many people have been supportive of me, and so of course I want to contribute. Of course I do." She still plans on pursuing her bachelor's degree. But along the way, Sidibe says, interpreting will provide her with more than just economic security for her and her now twelve-year-old daughter.

"Imagine coming in here. You have limited money to buy food and limited ability to communicate." Sidibe says. "When someone walks up and speaks to that person in their language, you can just see some of that stress leaving their face."

Measured in miles, Serafima Zaltsman's route to Found in Translation also spanned some four thousand miles. But measured in years, it lasted decades longer than Fatou Sidibe's. A few days after Zaltsman came to the United States as a Soviet Jewish refugee from St. Petersburg, Russia, in 1992, she sat down with a job counselor at a human services agency outside Boston.

Zaltsman, who was forty-six years old at the time, already spoke good English and was eager to find work.

The counselor asked her about her professional experience. There was a lot to talk about. Zaltsman had been a successful medical doctor in Russia. She had extensive training in orthopedics, emergency medicine, medical care during wartime, homeopathy, nutrition, and therapeutic massage. She had published articles in respected medical journals about Osgood-Schlatter disease, a knee condition that affects adolescents. She and her husband, a mathematician, had earned decent incomes. But after the disintegration of the Soviet Union in 1991, anti-Semitism and violence against Jews were on the rise. On the once peaceful crime-free streets of St. Petersburg, young men had hurled anti-Semitic slurs at Zaltsman's teenage son. State-sponsored anti-Semitism, notorious under the tsars and Josef Stalin, continued in various forms well into the 1980s. Like many observers at the time, Zaltsman and her family feared that the economic instability following the fall of the Soviet Union would escalate violence and systematic discrimination against Jews. It was time to get out, they decided. It would mean leaving everything—most of their possessions, their money, and their homes—behind to become refugees in the United States. The job counselor told Zaltsman she would help her put together a resume. The counselor also told Zaltsman things that she already knew: Do not wear low-cut shirts or short skirts to job interviews. Do not chew gum. A manager at the agency told her: "Don't wait for a job in medicine. Go apply at McDonald's."

Zaltsman never expected to work as a doctor in the United States right away. But she was dismayed to discover no way to get credit for her education, skills, and experience and no clear path to the additional training she would need to resume her career. She thought that becoming a nurse might be a good option. But this would have required starting over "with many years of education, in many cases learning many things that I already knew," which would cost money "we did not have."

So she applied for low-level jobs in the medical field. An opening for a phlebotomist—a person who draws blood—paid $8 an hour. Another, for a home health aide, paid a little more. She heard the same refrain from human resources staff: "One, I would need to have certification, and two, I was overqualified."

The temporary financial assistance her family had received upon arrival was about to run out. Zaltsman's husband was earning minimum wage pumping gasoline near their home in suburban Boston. (Later he would become a personal trainer at a gym.) So Zaltsman took the subway to a chain supermarket to apply for a job bagging groceries. On the way, she walked by the office of a visiting nurse association. She knew that visiting nurses made house calls to mostly elderly patients, so she stopped in and asked if they were hiring. She listened to the familiar refrain: she would need certification, and "anyway, you are overqualified."

But just then one of the nurses rushed in and interrupted the conversation. There was an emergency with a Russian-speaking patient across town, she said. They had no Russian speakers on staff.

"You do not need to pay me anything," Zaltsman told the women. "I would just like to help." She went and interpreted. The next day she was hired as an interpreter. The pay was just $8 an hour. But she worked forty hours a week and received health insurance coverage.

Later, Zaltsman would find better-paying work in research labs. One job ended when the lab moved to Italy. Another lab, at Boston's Beth Israel Hospital, lost its funding in 2013. And so, in her mid-sixties, Zaltsman once again found herself looking for a job. Just before getting laid off, she told staff members in Beth Israel's human resources office that she would be willing to "mop floors, work in the cafeteria, [or] empty the garbage" if only she could keep her health benefits. A program administrator at Beth Israel's human resources department, Babak Bagheral, said he would keep her offer in mind, but that she might consider applying to a program he admired, called Found in Translation.

Zaltsman took Bagheral's advice, though she left her age off her application. "I did not like being dishonest. But why would they want to make this kind of investment in an older person?" she says. A staff member at Found in Translation called her. "She told me, 'If you are worried that we would discriminate against you, we would not do that,'" Zaltsman recalls. "I told her my birth year. I still didn't think they'd be interested in me."

But they were very interested. She sat for an interview. She aced the language proficiency tests. "I still didn't think they would call," Zaltsman says. But they called. And from the start, Zaltsman has been among the most exuberant members of a class of particularly vibrant women.

During a show-and-tell on culturally based home remedies, several women offered samples of soothing oils, including argan from Morocco and baobab from Senegal. Some of them talked up the wonders of sage and other herbs for healing rashes, speeding up recovery from colds, or aiding depression. Zaltsman's contribution, though, inspired the greatest intrigue. Grinning, she stood up and displayed a brown leech in a jar of water. The women, some of them gasping and recoiling, others laughing, and all of them curious, passed the leech around. Leeches are useful for a lot of conditions, Zaltsman explained. But in the United States, they are an FDA-approved remedy to encourage healthy blood flow and prevent clots after skin grafts and amputations.

Looking back on her more than two decades in the United States and her twelve weeks at Found in Translation, Zaltsman says, "If I had come to this country and discovered something like Found in Translation when I first got here?" Tears come to her eyes. She pauses. "Well, I could have had a totally different life, a better life." She is not referring to money.

"Sure. A secure income would be nice," she says. "But no. It was the encouragement. It was that I was told, 'Yes, this country needs what you have. You have value.' This is what makes all the difference in the world."

—FORT WAYNE, IN—

Fort Wayne ★

RECLAMATION SPACE, RECLAIMING LIVES

In Fort Wayne, Indiana, Immigrants and Refugees Inspire New Hope for an Old Building in a Transformed City

About ninety years ago, an enterprising Greek immigrant named Jim Heliotes laid claim to his American dream on the corner of South Calhoun and West Pontiac Streets in Fort Wayne, Indiana. Heliotes endeavored to fill the empty lot on this downtown block with something beautiful, something lucrative, something beloved.

Heliotes made his dream come true. For several decades, his grand Rialto Theater, with a glazed terra-cotta facade, velvet-covered seats, and ornate chandeliers, drew sold-out crowds who watched Hollywood films, vaudeville performances, and concerts. With the Rialto as an anchor, this corridor of Fort Wayne's downtown kept prospering right on through the Great Depression. By 1940, hundreds of small shops, grocery stores, and a few large department stores filled the city's busy commercial center. During that time, the Rialto even added a balcony and another three hundred seats. But by the late 1960s, families began fleeing Fort Wayne in great numbers for newer developments in the suburbs. Mega movie complexes and strip malls followed the audiences and customers out there. And in 1967, the Heliotes family sold the Rialto.

For a few years, in the 1970s, the Rialto's new owners screened martial arts movies. When that failed, they tried showing Spanish-language films for the city's growing Mexican immigrant community. Neither venture proved lucrative, so they, too, sold the place. In the 1980s, new owners started screening pornographic movies. This finally brought in money. It also invited trouble in this God-fearing town. Residents and church officials—Fort Wayne's unofficial moniker is "A City of Churches"—picketed every day. In 1986, the county prosecutor's office sued to seize the Rialto, charging that the theater had become a site for gambling and prostitution, which indeed it had. After owners pled guilty to promoting prostitution, the theater closed in 1989. Fort Wayne had changed by then, too. As in other Rust Belt cities, lots of the factories had closed, including the biggest employer, International Harvester, which had made heavy-duty trucks and provided nearly eleven thousand jobs. For years to come, the formerly grand Rialto would sit on its formerly grand corner rotting from the inside out. Bricks crumbled. The roof leaked. Mold spread over the concrete. Rats roamed among the velvet seats.

"Somebody needs to do something with that place," Angie Harrison told her husband, Joe, as the couple drove by the Rialto one afternoon on their way to church.

Angie and Joe had moved back to Angie's native Fort Wayne in 2003 after living in southern California for a decade. They had settled close to the dilapidated theater, not far from Pontiac Street, the one neighborhood people had advised them to avoid. But Angie loved the character and detail of old houses, which were harder to find, not to mention more expensive, in the wealthier, whiter enclaves beyond the city center. She and Joe, who are both white, wanted to raise their school-age son and daughter amid the racial and cultural diversity to which they had become accustomed in California. In Fort Wayne, the Harrisons were thrilled to have Burmese, African American, Sudanese, Somali, Hispanic, and white working-class neighbors, whose children became their children's classmates and friends. As the months wore on, Angie discovered that her pull toward the Rialto was just as strong as ever. She found herself gazing at the place every time she drove past. Then one afternoon at church Angie and Joe started talking with fellow parishioners who said that they, too, had hopes for the Rialto. Jeff Jacobsen, a local insurance executive and father of four, along with his wife, Kristie, had been thinking very seriously about using the theater as a space to stage a play that Jeff had written. In the play, titled *Auditioning Jesus*, the main characters set out to produce a play about Jesus, but following a series of rejections, they are forced to put on the show in an old, decrepit theater. Then the director keeps choosing the wrong actor to play Jesus. Then Jesus himself auditions and gets the job. Being a carpenter, he begins to clean up the old theater and spread a message of redemption among community members.

Soon life began to imitate art. Jeff and Kristie had spotted the old Rialto and, like Angie Harrison, been charmed by its rough beauty and captivated by its history. Jacobsen and his pastor from Fellowship Missionary Church went down to talk with the Rialto's owner, who also owned a strip club in town. It turned out he was willing to let go of the eleven-thousand-square-foot Rialto, an adjacent former tobacco store, and the abutting parking lots for $160,000. (Jacobsen purchased the property and then, after the Reclamation Project earned its nonprofit status, transferred ownership to the organization.)

"To a lot of people the move to buy the Rialto seemed a little crazy, I suppose. But as soon as we embarked upon this, we knew that this place, this mission, was going to be about more than a play," Jacobsen said. "It was going to be about the community, reaching out to new members of the community."

The Rialto, by fits and starts, is again becoming a place that helps fulfill immigrants' aspirations and brings people together. Through volunteer labor and locally raised donations, by 2007 the Reclamation Project (TRP) had renovated about one thousand square feet and put its modest offices in part of that space. TRP operates with a part-time staff and a shoestring budget. Angie Harrison, now the executive director, has sacrificed a salary on and off during her tenure. Throughout the financial difficulties, TRP has managed to start and sustain an array of services and programs. Its Circle of Friends program pairs long-time Fort Wayne residents with newly arrived refugees and immigrants. The established residents act as guides and friends to the newcomers. Reclamation Project volunteers teach English to big groups who gather in immigrants' homes. Staff members offer document translation for a nominal fee. Staff, volunteers, refugees, and immigrants plant vegetable gardens. They host sewing and crafting classes for Burmese and African women. Through the Reclamation Products program, refugees and immigrants make and sell hats and mittens out of reclaimed materials. A used furniture store sits next door to the offices. Across the street, a Burmese family sells dumplings and other delicacies out of a small shop.

Reclamation Project staff members and volunteers envision the Rialto space as the World Café and Cultural Center. The World Café of the near future, Harrison explains, will include a small restaurant and an art gallery staffed by community residents. The theater, she and her staff members hope, will again host music, dance, and films that feature the myriad cultural contributions of people who live in Fort Wayne. More than anything, Harrison and others imagine a space for Fort Wayne's American-born residents to begin and deepen relationships with new immigrants—the Burmese, Sudanese, Somalis, Latinos and others—who have transformed the cultural landscape of this conservative midwestern city.

Fort Wayne is home to 255,000 people, including one of the largest communities of Burmese refugees in the United States. Churches and government agencies have settled more than four thousand Burmese here in waves since the late 1980s, following uprisings, violence, and persecution in Burma, the Southeast Asian nation that is also called Myanmar. Myo Myint, who lives in Fort Wayne, is the subject of the documentary *Burma Soldier*. Myint is a former Burmese soldier who became a prodemocracy activist and later found refuge in the United States.

Fort Wayne is also home to newer Sudanese and Somali refugee communities and a long-standing Latino population, largely of Mexican descent. In 2015, the Greater Fort Wayne Hispanic Chamber of Commerce celebrated its twenty-fifth anniversary. About 15 percent of the city's residents are African American, and 73 percent are white. There are indeed a lot of churches in Fort Wayne, as its nickname implies. Most are of the traditional midwestern Christian variety: Lutheran, Catholic, and Episcopalian. More recently, though, Buddhist monks from Burma have turned several otherwise ordinary ranch houses into temples on the city's south side. One, founded by members of the Mon ethnic group from Burma (there are seven principal ethnic groups in Myanmar and more than 130 subgroups), sits unceremoniously next to a gas station and convenience store. Burmese Muslims are building a new mosque on the south side, too, in the middle of a historically African American neighborhood. According to mosque members, this is the first new Burmese mosque built anywhere in the world since the 1970s.

In donated classroom space at Indiana University–Purdue University Fort Wayne, Kyaw Soe spends much of his Saturdays teaching the Burmese language to children who were born in Thai refugee camps or in the United States to Burmese refugee parents. A former student activist, Kyaw Soe fled Burma during the government crackdown that followed a nationwide uprising in the summer of 1988. That year, students, civil servants, ordinary people, and monks joined in protests against government curtailment of personal freedoms, economic mismanagement, police brutality, and the nation's one-party military rule. By August, hundreds of thousands of people had joined a general strike. As it had in years past, the military government responded violently, killing thousands of protesters and imposing martial law.

"America is our home. Fort Wayne is our home," says Kyaw Soe, who was part of the resistance movement working against the military junta in Burma. "But keeping alive our culture is important. This allows the parents to keep up good communication with their children. People lost their country. They do not have to lose their culture, too."

Soe explains that "the greatest sadness" that Burmese adults report to him is their "inability to communicate with their children." Burmese mothers and fathers, he says, "very much want their children to learn English. But to watch your child drift away and then to have no authority with that child is something that is not necessary. Children need their parents, and strong families provide this foundation. Children can build success and good relationships on top of those family relationships. It is what is so important in life. And we need to all support that."

Back at the Rialto, chips of paint spread like confetti across the floors. Holes in the plaster expose crumbling bricks. Blue and red plastic letters from the old marquee—piles of A's, B's, and so forth—sit in stacks amid planks and pipes. The air is damp and dusty. A big chunk of the ceiling is still torn up. But the roof has been fixed for some time now. A luminous aqua-blue dome decorated with gold-colored metal stars graces part of the ceiling above the theater's main floor. Contractors have told Angie Harrison that it would take upward of $1 million to fully restore the Rialto. For a small nonprofit, she acknowledges, raising that kind of money "creates a major challenge."

Though its staff and volunteers undoubtedly provide services, the Reclamation Project is different from a standard human service provider, and not only because it owns an interesting old theater and dreams big. "The goal is relationship," Angie Harrison says. "The point is reciprocity. Everyone has something to contribute. All of us can participate in giving and in receiving. We aren't interested in becoming a human service agency. We are interested in building relationships within a community." The vision for the World Café and the Reclamation Products program, Harrison points out, purposely builds on immigrants' strengths. It "showcases contributions," she says, rather than merely documenting needs and providing charity.

Even the Reclamation Project's English lessons are nonstandard. A lot of community-based organizations offer English classes, usually at their offices, a library, or a community center. But Reclamation Project teachers most often travel to students' homes, where a half dozen to a dozen adults gather to learn together. The standard teacher-student boundary is deliberately fuzzy, as friendships and even family-type relationships evolve. Reclamation Project volunteer Rick Piatt taught English to a group of Burmese men and women in one home for several years. Each time Piatt arrived, his hosts set out a single fresh flower and a pot of warm Burmese coffee on a table for him. One of the couples he taught adopted him as a grandfather figure for their son after the boy's grandfather died.

"There is something about going to people's homes and being in their space that makes all of this so much more meaningful," Piatt says. "You really do get to know each other. It's a sharing."

A few times a month, twentysomething Megan Painter travels across town to one of Fort Wayne's ubiquitous garden-style apartment complexes where Burmese refugees live. Inside the warm, dark apartment decorated with Southeast Asian tapestries, five women sit around a foldout table in a small breezeway turned classroom. Pungent, sweet aromas waft into the room from the galley kitchen about twenty feet away. The women are Rohingya Muslims, historically the most persecuted of all ethnic groups in Burma and, according to the United Nations, one of the most persecuted religious groups in the world. The Myanmar government does not even recognize Rohingya Muslims as citizens, insisting they are from neighboring Bangladesh even though Rohingya people have lived in Burma for at least several generations. They have suffered mass killings, rape, forced labor, and violent attacks on person and property by other ethnic groups in a largely Buddhist nation. Rohingya have found refuge in several nations, including the United States, India, and Thailand. The approximately one million stateless Rohingya remaining in Myanmar live segregated, apartheid-like, in the nation's Rakhine state on the western coast along the Bay of Bengal. According to the United Nations, about 140,000 Rohingya have been "internally displaced" and have been living in "deplorable" makeshift camps after clashes with Buddhists in 2012.

Over the two years Megan has worked with the Rohingya women in Fort Wayne, she's learned a lot about the women's lives and histories and they have learned about her. Megan has also learned to show up to this apartment hungry. She's fallen in love with Thai coffee, with curry and noodle soup. Having left Burma as youngsters, most of the women here spent their childhoods and young adult years in refugee camps in Thailand.

"We love to see Megan," says one of the women, Sein Tom Be. "We like to feed her, too." Before class begins, another woman, Ma Nige, urges Megan to practice a few Burmese words. One sounds something like "chit-tey."

"Ah yes. I know that one," Megan tells Ma Nige confidently. "It means 'love.' That was one of the first words you taught me."

In 2015, Harrison and the staff and volunteers at TRP widened their imaginative lenses again and partnered with the city to create a development plan for what's been designated the SoCal—for South Calhoun Street—area. They hope to benefit from development in the central downtown area and attract more commercial and government investment to their part of town. But whatever changes come, Angie Harrison says, will reflect the desires, hopes, and dreams of the small business owners and residents in their remarkably diverse part of town. Harrison knows that "development begets development" and that "investments beget more investments." But this is about more than money and socioeconomic ascension.

"The idea is that the Rialto will be the anchor, and of course we love that idea," Harrison says. "We see this work as part of our bridge-building efforts. The people who are here, who've made this place their home, who have already invested here, need to be the ones who have a voice and benefit from whatever happens." To that end, TRP hosts community conversations and meets with Asian, Latino, and African American business owners to cohere a group committed to reinvigorating the neighborhood on their own terms.

"This stretch of street has had its share of hard times—all kinds of challenges through history. And it's also a place with so many assets," with that incredibly rich diversity and energy being one of those strengths, Harrison says. "To do this right, to make sure that everyone is included and has a voice in the future of this area? Well, that's going to take a while. Just like when you are trying to renovate an old theater. You need patience. But I can tell you that we are staying right here on the corner to contribute, to be a part of what the future brings."

DURHAM, NC

WEALTH FOR EVERYONE

A North Carolina Credit Union Serves a Growing Immigrant Population and Creates a Safer, More Prosperous Community

Not long after he arrived in Durham, North Carolina, in 1996, Marcelino Varela learned a lesson that would prove valuable in his adopted city: always be ready to sprint.

He was sixteen, with a sixth-grade education, when he followed his father from Puebla, Mexico, to the booming Research Triangle. His father set up banquets at Durham's downtown convention center, and Varela got hired to work alongside him. "My dad had a car, but he had two jobs," Varela recalls. "There wasn't a lot of bus service, so I had to walk. During the daytime, it was OK. But sometimes at nighttime, it was dangerous. A lot of times I had to run, and people would run behind me. I was eighteen, nineteen years old, so"—he pauses and laughs nervously—"you can run fast."

Varela was an attractive mark. Even though he had a bank account, many of the young Latino men arriving in Durham during the 1990s did not. That meant they carried a lot of cash with them. Some were afraid of the police—either because of their legal status or because of the reputation of the police back home—and reluctant to report armed robberies. During those years, you could rarely turn on the TV without hearing terrible news, such as the 1997 murder of Jose Orellana, a Salvadoran immigrant who was gunned down as he was walking to a convenience store near Duke University. "I was scared," Varela says. His first instinct was understandable: "Go back to my country, never come back."

John Herrera, who, at the time worked at Duke's Center for International Studies, was all too aware of the crime wave targeting recent immigrants. In 1994, he had founded El Pueblo, a community building organization best known for its annual Latino festival. Herrera knew that building bridges between communities was critical: even though Durham bulged with newcomers, many of its neighborhoods remained hostile places for those who arrived speaking Spanish and looking for blue-collar jobs.

"People were being robbed and killed because they were walking banks," says Herrera, who himself had emigrated from Costa Rica. "Criminals knew that the easiest way to make money is you rob a Mexican or Latino immigrant any Friday afternoon on payday and you get cash. And better yet, they don't even report the crime to the police." It wasn't just that immigrants didn't trust banks with their money. "Financial institutions didn't see them as viable customers," Herrera says. "They thought it was not a good business strategy to target these folks because they were low-balance accounts, poor working-class people. Who wants them, right?"

Those robberies provided the initial spark for what's become a national model of immigrant self-empowerment with the Durham-based Latino Community Credit Union (LCCU). Launched in 2000 as a safe place for people of Hispanic descent to deposit their paychecks, it has blossomed into a full-service bilingual operation with 55,000 member-owners, eleven branches across North Carolina, and $105 million in assets. It has a dedicated program of outreach to those without much wealth or financial sophistication, and it has developed an ambitious education program to increase its members' know-how. As the Latino community has become more established—and readier to buy homes and start businesses—the credit union has kept pace with those needs. About 90 percent of members are people who earn low incomes, and about 70 percent are people who had previously been "unbanked"—that is, without any savings or checking account or loans.

"We're really taking people who have been systematically marginalized and helping to incorporate them into the mainstream," says Erika Bell, LCCU's vice president for strategy and services. "I love the credit union philosophy and model, but even amongst credit unions we're unique in that we have such a very pointed mission to incorporate low-income and traditionally unbanked people into the system." In pursuing that mission, LCCU has met with a success far greater than its founders envisioned in the thick of the crisis.

When they first conceived of the idea of creating a credit union, the first instinct of Durham's Latino leaders in the 1990s was to gather together anyone with power: police, city officials, bankers, nonprofit leaders, Catholic and Episcopal clergy. They also reached out to existing credit unions, including the Durham based Self-Help, which lends to women, people of color, and rural communities. "They asked us: 'What do you guys need to solve this problem?'" Herrera recalls. "Our response was we need our own financial institution. Plan B, we were ready to settle for a bilingual branch of Self-Help. I thought that would solve the problem. But our parents taught us always to ask for the stars in the sky. If you don't get that, you get whatever is below that.

"And these folks"—the other credit unions—"said yes to all these requests," Herrera continues. "We said: 'We need you guys to commit to help us, coach us, mentor us. We don't want this to be a hit-and-run relationship. We want to learn how to bank our community. We want money, we need technology, we need a lot of things.' And they committed. They even brought the regulators to a meeting to guide us. So to our surprise, not only did we get what we asked for, but we got more."

The North Carolina State Employees' Credit Union lent access to its enormous infrastructure; it now provides back-office support such as technology and accounting. It also offered high-level executives as coaches. Self-Help shared its deep expertise—and also hired Herrera to focus exclusively on building a Latino credit union. (He's now a senior vice president at Self-Help.) The North Carolina Minority Support Center, a nonprofit that partners with community development credit unions, particularly ones in African American communities, identified foundations and other resources to finance LCCU's start-up. Knowing how many Latinos were unbanked, LCCU's founders wondered whether anyone would show up to deposit their money. "We knew people had been ripped off by banks in their home countries," Herrera says. "We knew the majority of members had never had a bank account back at home. What would make us believe that they were going to trust us here in the United States?" Still, the founders set an aggressive goal of adding five hundred new members a year.

"That number got thrown to the wind in the first month of existence," he recalls. During opening week in 2000, several members of the clergy told their congregations about the credit union. "By the next day, we started seeing the lines of people forming, and it's been nonstop ever since." The National Federation of Community Development Credit Unions calls LCCU the fastest-growing community development credit union in the United States.

It was going to be a challenge, to put it mildly, to build a credit union whose core membership is accustomed to stashing cash in their mattresses. "You find people that come from rural areas where there are not just no financial institutions: There is no electricity, there is no running water in these communities in Guatemala, or in Honduras, or in some areas of Mexico," says Luis Pastor, LCCU's president and CEO. "So what do we expect when they come here, if they never have been exposed to that and they don't feel especially welcome in institutions here?" The key, Pastor and his colleagues realized, would be education, starting at the most rudimentary level. It's important, he says, that a member "not feel embarrassed because you don't know what a checking account is."

LCCU developed a free workshop series to teach its members basic financial management concepts: using debit cards, building credit, shopping for cars, writing household budgets, buying houses. The credit union offers the seven-week series three times a year at each of its eleven branches. LCCU plans to expand the program to include topics such as insurance, investing, and running small businesses. For those who can't attend the workshops, the credit union produced its own educational videos that play at the branches throughout the day. These formal education programs dovetail with policies designed to improve access. Business is conducted in Spanish and English. Minimum deposits are kept low ($10 to start a savings account).

Interest rates on accounts are the same for all members, so as not to favor wealthier depositors. No one is allowed to walk into a branch for the first time and merely fill out an application; staff members meet with new members for thirty to forty-five minutes to assess their needs. "At the very beginning, we saw member service representatives going with members hand by hand and telling them, 'This is the way you introduce a card to the ATM. This is the way you key your PIN. It's secret; don't keep it in your wallet,'" says Vicky Garcia, LCCU's vice president of operations.

What's more, photo identification from any country is acceptable, as long as it's accompanied by proof of address in the United States. For example, a new member can provide a foreign passport combined with a local utility bill. "We are not Immigration," Pastor says. "Financial institutions shouldn't be checking the status of people. There are almost one hundred different types of visas in this country. Are you providing . . . training to all your employees? Well, then don't ask for identification, because you may get in a place where you get really lost."

Not only do many banks have more stringent ID requirements, but some have double standards for different services, says Garcia. "Sometimes [the bank] opens the account, but the moment they need a loan: 'No, no, no, you don't qualify.' They take your money, but they won't make you a loan."

As LCCU put down roots in North Carolina, it developed enough credibility to convince immigrants that hiding their money at home was an unnecessary risk. "It was great when you were in the branch and somebody came with a jar that still smells of earth," says Pastor. "It had been in a ditch for years in the backyard. And people come with $10,000, $20,000, $30,000 in bills, and this is their life savings. This is one of the most rewarding moments: when people put everything that they own, everything that they've been fighting for, under your custody and say, 'I trust you.'"

When Marcelino Varela first joined the credit union—he and some friends saw the sign outside its Durham branch—he knew nothing about personal finances. "We have a tradition in Mexico," he says. "When we're younger, we work and we give our parents the money [to manage]. My dad took care of my money until I was nineteen." At LCCU he opened checking and savings accounts, and a staff member explained that he could build credit by taking out small personal loans. The first $500 loan he banked just to repay, and that eventually qualified him for two car loans. Varela has a girlfriend who has children. He also has a job as a manager at a private dining club.

"I'm thinking to buy a house," he says. Like Varela, many of LCCU's members have progressed along the financial sophistication continuum. So have the credit union's products, which are designed as affordable alternatives to the predatory lending practices that have forced many low-income Americans into debt spirals. LCCU began with small personal and used car loans, moved on to larger loans for new cars and SUVs, and then added home loans. One mortgage product launched in 2004 was aimed at members without credit histories—LCCU has developed nontraditional ways of measuring creditworthiness. A few years ago, it launched its first small-business loans, which currently max out at $10,000.

"Again, small steps," Garcia says. "We want to grow it to $50,000. That is the goal for this year."

As LCCU grew, it started attracting U.S.-born depositors drawn to its social mission. It also attracted non-Latino immigrants and refugees from countries such as Kenya, Myanmar, and Bhutan. Some, like their Latino neighbors, had been excluded from the banking system. Credit union vice presidents Garcia and Bell have both heard stories about banks rejecting unfamiliar documents presented by refugees—even though those papers were issued by the federal government. Some of those non-Latino immigrants were also drawn by the credit union's flexible view of creditworthiness. (This view has paid off, by the way; LCCU's loan default rate is one-fourth the national average for credit unions.)

Lima Marchan, who came to the United States from Trinidad in 1989, was working at a Durham hotel when she ran into financial difficulties and had to file for bankruptcy protection. She was also suffering from health problems: the fast pace of hotel work left her without time to control her diabetes. At a friend's suggestion, she started her own business cleaning homes—and within three years had enough clients to hire her first employee. What Marchan didn't have was the capital to upgrade her equipment; she was using the same vacuum cleaner with which she cleaned her own home. It was no way to run a business. Marchan went to her bank. It had been five years since the bankruptcy filing, but a loan officer told her she would not be creditworthy for another two more.

In confidence, a bank employee advised Marchan to join the Latino Community Credit Union and apply for a business loan there. "I'm not Hispanic," she recalls telling him. "How am I going to get in there?"

"It's not only for Hispanics," he replied. "It's for everybody."

So she opened an account. A loan officer asked, "What do you want?"

"I need a loan," Marchan said, but she was only joking, she says.

"How much?" he replied.

With the $5,000 she borrowed, Marchan bought vacuum cleaners, dusters, polishers, and cleaning fluids. She expects to qualify for a larger loan, which will help her buy a truck and expand her business to include trash removal, lawn care, and pressure washing. She also attended the credit union's classes, which she says helped her avoid repeating the mistakes of her past.

"They make me focus on the value of the dollar [and how] not to abuse credit cards," Marchan says. "I got to learn how to build my credit." During those few weeks, "I learned more about managing my money than in the twenty years that I'm living here in the States."

More than anything, Marchan feels a sense of belonging at LCCU. With mainstream banks, "you go there, you put your money in, 'Hello, bye, see you next week,'" she says. "This one is not like that. You come in there, and from the back you will hear Geraldo or Manuel: 'Hey, Lima, Doña Lima, ¿cómo estás?' They're not only employees. They're like a home where you walk into, and they may not offer you food, but they offer you good services with the biggest smile. It's like a nice big house."

There's no precise way to measure the credit union's impact on crime, though the frenzy of robberies of Latinos has clearly subsided. It's hard to separate out all the reasons for this decline. But a study by the University of Virginia Darden School of Business cites LCCU's presence as a key factor. The study found a 14 percent drop in robberies of Durham County's Latinos from 1999 (just before LCCU's opening) to 2002. During that same period, North Carolina's other counties averaged a slight rise.

The researchers repeated the study in four other counties with LCCU branches and found similar results in three. Other factors—the size of the Latino population and the number of cops on the street—did not diminish the strength of their findings. The drop in crime triggered a rise in property values, the analysts concluded: "By 2008, LCCU establishments had apparently contributed to the appreciation of $9.8 billion in taxable real-estate value."

"We're saving lives," says Pastor, the CEO.

But it's not just about crime anymore, and not just about Latinos. By reducing robberies, creating entrepreneurs, and even stimulating property value increases, the Latino Community Credit Union is creating wealth for everyone who lives in its midst.

—HAZLETON,PA—

Hazleton ★

WE ARE FROM HAZLETON

A Baseball Celebrity Helps Bring His Divided Pennsylvania Hometown Together

At the end of the 2010 Major League baseball season, Tampa Bay Rays manager Joe Maddon returned to the former coal mining community of Hazleton, Pennsylvania, where he had grown up. He sat on a child-size folding chair at a holiday potluck party hosted by a Dominican mother of three who ran a day care center out of her home. Spanish conversation flowed around him. Children ran about, weaving among the adults, who talked, laughed, and shared cuisine from the Dominican Republic, Guatemala, and Peru. Merengue music blared.

Maddon, who is Italian (formerly Maddonini, on his father's side) and Polish (on his mother's side), had over the years developed an affinity for Latin culture through his relationships with baseball players from Latin America and the Caribbean. As a coach, of course, he had no choice but to get players from different countries and cultures and linguistic backgrounds to work as a team. These days, Maddon, who grew up in a small apartment over his father's plumbing shop, is known for his quirky intellectual curiosity, his open and personable manner, and his

love of fine wines. Back in the 1980s, he learned his nearly fluent Spanish from his friend Dickie Thon, the Puerto Rican
shortstop, when they were both with the California/Anaheim
Angels organization. Maddon had been a bench coach for the
Angels and interim manager there in 1996 and 1999. (In 2015,
Maddon would move on from the Tampa Bay Rays organization to become manager of the Chicago Cubs.)

Joe Maddon is a celebrity in the sports world and a sought-
after spokesperson and benefactor. So you might think he would
want privacy most of all when he came back home to visit with
family at Christmas. But he had come to this particular party
quite on purpose. Curious and concerned, he had asked his
cousin, Elaine Maddon Curry, to introduce him to people from
the growing Latino community that had been moving to Hazleton since the early 2000s.

"Where are the Latinos?" Maddon asked his cousin. "Because I don't see them."

In 2006, Hazleton, a city of 25,000 people, had become the
first municipality in the nation to pass its own anti-immigration
law in the form of several ordinances. Partly as a result of this,
Maddon Curry explained, lots of Latino families she knew were
feeling unwelcome and tended to stay close to home.

The down-at-the-heels city of Hazleton sits in northeast
Pennsylvania's Luzerne County, about fifty miles north of Al-
lentown in what used to be coal country. The unemployment
rate here was nearly 11 percent in late 2014, compared with
6 percent nationally and 6 percent in Pennsylvania. Shuttered
buildings and storefronts are common, as is nostalgia about Hazleton's prosperous past. Hazleton has long been a gateway city
for immigrants. Following the Civil War, jobs generated by the
coal industry and railroad expansion attracted people from all
over the world.

Irish and Germans arrived first, in the 1850s. Later, immigrants arrived from Poland and Italy in a migration that continued into the early 1920s. In coal's heyday, which ended by the

late 1950s, Hazleton's population was more than twice what it is now. (Joe Maddon's paternal grandfather, an Italian immigrant, worked in the nearby coal mines.) As the nation moved toward oil, decent-paying jobs moved away, as did the younger generations and commercial investment. Low-wage jobs in meatpacking and big corporate warehouses have more recently replaced the higher-wage work of the greatly diminished coal and railroad industries. The low-wage work attracted a new wave of immigrants, mostly from the Dominican Republic and other Spanish-speaking countries.

"It is not as expensive as New York," explains Maribel Hernandez, owner of a small local restaurant, Mi Casa, which opened in 2012 and features American staples like pizza and chicken nuggets alongside Latin dishes such as rabo encendido (oxtail stew). Hernandez moved to Hazleton in 2005, she says, because of its relatively lower rents and because it seemed safe.

For the first time since the 1940s, Hazleton experienced growth in the past decade. From 2001 to 2013, the population grew about 9 percent to 25,300 residents. In that same period, according to the U.S. Census, the share of Hazleton's population that was Latino also grew—from 5 to 38 percent of all residents. This means all of the city's population growth is due to its Latino population. Without Latinos, the city would have most certainly continued to lose population as older residents died and people moved away. It would have undoubtedly suffered even more than it already has, since a diminishing tax base and commercial disinvestment nearly always accompany population loss.

Jamie Longazel, an assistant professor of sociology at the University of Dayton, grew up in Hazleton and has conducted intensive research on the city's anti-immigrant ordinance's origins and aftermath. His studies reveal that Hazleton's Latinos got blamed for an economic downturn that was, in reality, caused by a complex mix of far more powerful forces. As the economy worsened, Hazleton officials in recent years did what other similarly situated desperate urban leaders did: they offered tax breaks to corporations that offered low-wage jobs in return. The jobs could not lift people out of poverty, and tax breaks shrank the revenues available for city services. Meanwhile, ordinary people in Hazleton, Longazel says, "sensed more of a general decline, feeling as though the city is suffering in some way." He adds: "People were not talking about this. Immigrants were made the scapegoat."

The 2006 murder of a white Hazleton resident, Longazel says, "just blew everything up." Initially police arrested two Latinos for the crime, only to drop the charges later. Longazel's interviews with Hazleton residents show that mounting anti-immigrant sentiments took root and spread rapidly and thoroughly in this down-on-its-luck community, leading to passage of the controversial ordinances. As is true generally across the United States, though, undocumented immigrants had not increased crime in Hazleton. Longazel has noted that between 2001 (the year Latinos began arriving in high numbers in Hazleton) and 2006 (the year the ordinances passed) undocumented people accounted for just 0.25 percent of arrests.

In 2007, Maddon Curry and two Latino fathers had founded an organization called Concerned Parents, which provides an array of services, including interpreting for parent-teacher conferences, homework help, and English classes, mainly for immigrant families. She told Maddon that the city's Latino immigrants had retreated in fear and that, for the most part, Latino social lives went on in small apartments and multifamily homes. Families did come out for church, or to drop off and pick up their children at school. Maddon Curry also said she had seen more and more Latino adults participating in Concerned Parents English classes over the years. But typically, Maddon Curry explained, Hazleton's newcomers were wary and distrustful of people outside their social circles.

For Latinos in Hazleton, distrust was a sensible reaction.

Passed by a 6-to-1 vote, the highly publicized 2006 ordinances barred landlords from knowingly renting to unauthorized immigrants, required employers to verify their workers' immigration status, made it a violation to provide "services" beyond medical care to undocumented immigrants, and declared English as the city's official language. The measures won praise from conservative talk radio hosts and condemnation from national immigrant rights, civil rights, and labor organizations. The city also got sued by a coalition of civil rights organizations led by the American Civil Liberties Union In 2007, a federal judge struck down the local ordinance. The city appealed. At the time of Maddon's visit, in 2010, the future of the ordinances was unclear.

Back home in Hazleton during that period, Maddon became dispirited by conversation with local folks who quite often blamed immigrants for Hazleton's economic decline. But during the same visit, the potluck party with immigrant families had deeply pleased him. The flavors, the music, and the language may have been different from the Italian- and Polish-centered celebrations of his youth. But the warmth of community and family and friends, the easy banter, the centrality of family, and the ethnic pride felt familiar.

At the potluck, he turned to his cousin Elaine Maddon Curry and told her: "This is how we grew up. This is it, right here."

"That was my seminal moment." Maddon would later recall. "We're the same, just speak a different language . . . the Slovak, the Polish, the Irish, the Italians. We all started the same."

As he was leaving to head back to his life and his high-pressure job in Tampa, Maddon told Maddon Curry and her husband, Bob Curry, that he wanted to "do something to repair what had been damaged here." Bob Curry recalls: "He was really very deeply concerned about this division that he saw in a community that he just loves so much."

After consultation with the Currys and other community members, Maddon decided he would help fund and, most important, lend his voice and celebrity to start the Hazleton Integration Project, an array of events, programs, and services known locally now as HIP. Since that visit back in 2010, Maddon has played a central role in fund-raising. He attracted the Cal Ripken Jr. Foundation and scores of other donors who've given money to the Project. He's also signed up big-name baseball greats including Yogi Berra, Tino Martinez, and Carlos Peña as active spokespeople for the cause. Maddon has been out front during several packed public events where he has urged members of the Latino immigrant community and the white community to get to know each other and figure out, together, how to foster prosperity in the economically eviscerated city they share. In 2012, Maddon backed the purchase of a former Catholic school to house the Hazleton One Community Center, which became HIP's headquarters. The center hosts social events, cultural celebrations, potlucks, and a wide range of sports and recreation programs, and it organizes a homework help center for children. English classes and citizenship classes, offered through the Concerned Parents organization, have moved over to the former Catholic school, along with a popular Saturday storytelling program for children. Educators also offer Spanish courses for residents and involve many members of the immigrant community in organizing, teaching, and assisting with instruction.

Many municipalities have community centers. And an increasing number of cities have opened welcoming centers for immigrants in recent years. But Hazleton One is something else entirely.

"This is not a place that is only for immigrants. And it is not just an open gym. The very explicit goal of this place and of this effort is clear: it is to bring two currently much separated communities together," says Bob Curry, HIP's board president. "Yes, we will provide particular services, but the larger mission of integration will guide us in everything that we do. Services are one thing. Integration is quite another. . . . It's a longer-range goal."

In late 2012, Maddon had flown up from Florida with some of his ball players to announce Hazleton One's opening. At the new center, he shared the stage with the former first baseman Tino Martinez, who had played for the New York Yankees and for Tampa Bay. Many of the kids and grown-ups clutched baseballs they hoped to get signed.

"We want to get kids off the street. . . . We want sports, culinary, drama clubs. Everything we can imagine and afford, that's what we want to do. We're opening this for the entire community. This is for everybody," Maddon told the standing-room-only crowd. "For all our brothers and sisters."

Sports celebrity philanthropy is often generous. But the good causes our athletic heroes champion are rarely controversial. They tend more toward helping children who have cancer or donating sports equipment to the poor. Expanding services for people who may be undocumented and encouraging racial and ethnic healing do not usually make the list. But Maddon's quest for unity in his fractured hometown has, according to HIP organizers, received "only some minor complaints."

The Hazleton One Community Center is also the new home of Concerned Parents, the five-year-old grassroots effort that Maddon's cousin Elaine Maddon Curry founded in partnership with Eugenio Sosa, who is now Hazleton One's executive director. From the start, Joe Maddon has stressed that he sees his job as providing the financial resources, credibility, and attention he can while "entrusting" the on-the-ground work and larger vision to "people who know what they are doing." This includes Sosa, Hazleton One's executive director.

Originally from the Dominican Republic, Sosa came to the United States in 1989 and to Hazleton in 2006. The father of three children in the public schools, he worked with Elaine Maddon Curry to establish the volunteer interpreting, English classes, and citizenship classes that quickly grew into Concerned Parents.

"This is following our dream," Sosa says. "We are starting with the children. . . . They are going to be spending time together, playing together, learning together, going to each other's houses, learning about different cultures, how different people celebrate. It is just a great opportunity."

The children who spend time at Hazelton One Community Center, Sosa hopes, "will end up bringing their parents along on this journey, sharing that space, and over time these perceptions will be gone. We know it may be a longer process with some of the adults, but with the children, it happens so fast if you give them the chance and that space, which we have now."

Jamie Longazel stresses that demographically changing communities like Hazleton would benefit from efforts such as HIP that focus on relationship building and stronger cross-cultural alliances among working people who, he writes, "can withstand anti-immigrant scare tactics." Having moved recently from the Bronx, Rafael Polanco, who is of Dominican descent, owns a small grocery supply business in Hazleton. He welcomes the opportunities for integration that HIP is making possible. "That is the step needed to get us all involved, all together," says Polanco, who attended Maddon's press conference. "We can't operate pulling for one community or the other. It has to be one. I think this gets us closer to that."

Sitting in an English class at the local YMCA, Rafael Castillo says he discovered Concerned Parents services the way most immigrants do—through word of mouth from friends and relatives. He sat among five women: one from Colombia, another from Mexico, and three, like him, from the Dominican Republic. Drawn to the city two years ago by family and a job in a chocolate factory, Castillo heard about long waiting lists for English classes. But he added his name anyway.

"I have to learn the language, it's only right," Castillo says during a break in volunteer instructor Beth Turnbach's class.

Turnbach says she wanted to be a counterforce to the negative comments she has heard her fellow Hazleton residents make about Latinos. She says she decided that teaching Hazleton's newest residents was the best way for her to do that.

On an old overpass, a spray-painted (and misspelled) slur, "Spick," is fading. Not long from now, it will barely be visible. Signs of progress along Hazleton's Wyoming Street, downtown, feel more enduring. A several-generations-old sporting goods store sits amid the newer Dalia's Salon and other Dominican-owned businesses, including Luis's barbershop and a tax preparation service.

Not too far from downtown is a Mexican restaurant where Maddon and his wife, Jaye, sat down to eat a few years ago. Recognizing Maddon's celebrity, a cook came over and greeted the people at the table. Maddon, familiar with Mexico's geography, asked him in Spanish: "Where are you from?" The cook, though, seemed perplexed by the question. "I'm from Hazleton," he answered in English. Maddon found instant inspiration in this miscommunication, and he voiced an idea. Perhaps prominently placed billboards with pictures of culturally diverse groups of Hazleton's residents, he suggested to Jaye, might be a constructive step in the healing process.

Those billboards went up in 2013. That same year, the U.S. Court of Appeals for the Third Circuit ruled that Hazleton's ordinances related to immigrants, housing, and employment were unconstitutional. The city appealed again, this time to the U.S. Supreme Court, which refused to hear the cases. This meant that the Appeals Court ruling stood and Hazleton's ordinances did not go into effect.

During a pro-immigrant Unity March organized by HIP and other residents in 2014, some marchers carried smaller poster-size copies of the billboards Maddon had envisioned. They amplified the Mexican-born cook's simple message: "We are from Hazleton."

IDAHO

★ Boise

GARDENS GONE GLOBAL

In Boise, Idaho, Refugee Farmers Reconnect to the Land and Pass On Old Traditions in a New Place

Friday nights in spring, summer, and early fall, when many of her fellow high school seniors are getting ready for parties or heading out to a football game, seventeen-year-old Fatuma Mnongerwa spends hours mixing, flattening, and then cutting dozens of pieces of dough into small squares. She spoons a savory mixture of spices, vegetables, and meats onto each piece and pinches them into triangular pockets. Fatuma's mother, Amina, works alongside her. Amina, with help from Fatuma and several of her other six children, grew the herbs, potatoes, carrots, onions, and other vegetables that go into these sambusas, a beloved, traditional Somali snack. On Saturday morning Amina, Fatuma, and Fatuma's brother Chubangu, a high school junior, will head out to the Capital City Public Market, where they will drop the sambusas into a deep fryer and sell them along with carefully selected fruits and vegetables from their garden.

"I absolutely love doing this. It reminds you that your family is a team," Fatuma says. She came to Boise when she was seven years old. Before moving here, Fatuma had lived in a Kenyan refugee camp after her parents fled the violence and chaos of Somalia's civil war that began in 1991. With aspirations to be a lawyer, Fatuma is consumed with applying to colleges this year and competing on the track team at Boise's Capital High School. But no matter where she goes or what she does, she says, "I will always be able to find peace and just a feeling of amazement" from "looking at dirt that's empty—just dirt and then planting something and seeing it grow." Fatuma gets great satisfaction, too, from watching her mother start her own business and continue Somali food traditions in the United States.

"I have no feeling about Somalia. My mother has those memories that can keep her connected, but I guess I'd say I'm pretty American. Somali American, but yeah, American," Fatuma says. "I feel connected to Somali culture in other ways, though. There's always food, the gardening. Those things my mother gave me. It means that it never gets lost."

Fatuma's mother, Amina, decided to make a go of her small business venture back in 2010, soon after she began helping to cultivate a garden plot her husband, Yussuf, had obtained through a local project called Global Gardens. Operated by the nonprofit Idaho Office for Refugees, the Global Gardens initiative provides donated land, equipment, and a variety of technical supports to farmers who are members of Boise's strikingly diverse and sizable refugee community. Founded in 2004, Global Gardens staff acquired and now help maintain eleven donated pieces of land in and around the city—on synagogue and church properties, city land, and other locations. A single two-acre farm, cut into quarter-acre plots, accommodates seven refugee farmers. About three hundred refugees, including many large families, participate in the program. Some of the gardeners and farmers grow food for themselves and their families. About a dozen "market" farmers, like Amina, sell their food at the weekly seasonal farmers' market, through the Global

Gardens community-supported agriculture (CSA) program, or both. About seventy CSA subscribers in and around Boise pay for a share of the Global Gardens harvest. Every week from late May until the first of October, the subscribers pick up fresh fruit and vegetables at different locations around the city.

After enhancing her gardening skills, improving her English, and building her self-confidence, Amina was cultivating her own Global Gardens plot by 2011 and managing her own stand at the farmers' market, contributing to the family's income. Soon after that, she expanded by selling homemade sambusas alongside the cabbage, lettuce, tomatoes, green beans, squash, and herbs she and her family grew. People kept buying her vibrant veggies and fruit, but the sambusas were by far the biggest hit. Now, even long after the growing season is over, Amina takes sambusa orders from friends and acquaintances, from customers she's met at the farmers' market, and for events at the local Islamic center. She is also a reliable and popular supplier for the Global Gardens CSA program.

After a long, glorious stretch of brilliant sun and seventy-degree early fall weather, it's cloudy, a little drizzly, and raw for the Saturday morning opening of the farmers' market. Fatuma, her brother Chubangu, and her mother, Amina, arrange piles of lettuce, radishes, brilliant red tomatoes of many sizes, and fragrant cilantro. Fatuma positions a colorful sign out front reading AMINA'S SAMBUSAS. The chilly weather, Fatuma speculates, will drive people to the hot chocolate booth—and, she hopes, to her mother's warm, satisfying, spicy sambusas.

Every Saturday morning from April through mid-December crowds flock to Boise's farmers' market, where some 150 vendors set up booths. The market, which first opened in 1994, has grown over the years to span four city blocks in the shadow of Idaho's grand state capitol building. There are makers of jalapeño wine, potters selling hand-thrown coffee cups and dinner plates, artisans selling custom leather belts and wind chimes made from silver spoons. Two men sell Kobe steaks near an organic juice bar, where a young person in jogging gear pulls out a crisp $20 bill for three large drinks. There is Mexican hot chocolate with chili pepper, steaming tamales, and Dutch-inspired stroopwafel cookies, too. Within minutes of the official nine-thirty opening, parents with high-end strollers, couples of all ages, and many toddlers, school-age kids, and teenagers crowd the car-free streets. By eleven-thirty there's a line of five people waiting for Amina's sambusas.

Fatuma likes people-watching and chatting with passersby at the market. But she especially loves introducing new customers to their first-ever sambusas. They are first crisp and then chewy, with an intense yet comforting, instantly warming flavor burst of tender onions, cardamom, cinnamon, juicy beef, and melt-in-your mouth potatoes.

"Isn't it just so, so good?" Fatuma asks a woman who has just bitten into her first-ever sambusa.

The woman's mouth is too full for her to answer at first, but she soon says. "Oh. My. God. What is in this? This is, like, amazing." The young woman buys another sambusa. "I'm gonna get this for my boyfriend. Oh my God, he's going to love it! Umm, so, these are African? I mean, they are from Africa?"

"Yes!" Fatuma says. "It is a very traditional recipe, yes! We are from Somalia. Well, we are from Boise! But yes, yes, this food is African."

Food- and agriculture-based programs have proven a popular and effective means of integration for refugees and immigrants not just in Idaho but also in Maine, Missouri, California and Massachusetts. Idaho, famous for its bountiful potato crop, is an especially fitting setting for such an approach. Nearly 12 million acres here are used for farming purposes. Agriculture, still a substantial part of Idaho's economy, provides more than 100,000 jobs in a state and nation dominated by service industries. The federal government, through its Office of Refugee Resettlement, began funding programs similar to the Global Gardens initiative in 1998. The U.S. Department of Agriculture also provides small grants to local agriculture-based programs aimed at integrating and assisting immigrants and refugees. Global Gardens survives on a combination of these federal grants, combined with local grants, individual donations, and the bit of money the CSA subscriptions bring in. Federal funders tend to focus on the economic benefits of farming for refugees and stress the programs' role in "self-sufficiency." But for most of the refugee gardeners and farmers in Idaho, making lots of money is not realistic and a bit beside the point.

Some of Boise's refugee farmers, such as Amina, do end up making money from their work while at the same time improving their English skills, sharpening their business acumen, and increasing their engagement with the wider Boise community. Typically, though, market farming "provides really only a supplemental income, money to make life a little easier, pay a few more bills," says Global Gardens' high-energy coordinator, Katie Painter, who developed a love for agriculture after spending time on her grandparents' dairy farm in Pennsylvania. As a Peace Corps volunteer, Painter had worked with cotton farmers and corn growers in Paraguay and before that with cocoa bean growers in Brazil. Her broad experiences, internationally and in the United States, have made Painter pragmatic about how much money working the land can really provide.

Even the most financially successful refugee farmers, Painter says, are either mothers caring for young children during the day or people who have "very low-paying, often very hard, physical jobs outside the home." For most of the immigrants and refugees she works with, the benefits of farming and gardening, she says, "unfortunately can't be measured very easily." Some refugee farmers, Painter says, grow food to provide healthy and culturally familiar vegetables and fruits that they cannot find in stores around Idaho. For others, "it becomes a way for families to share something during a time in which there can be that threat of disconnection, when you have the young people in the family learning English and beginning that integration,"

Painter says. "Maybe the parents and the grandparents are at a different stage of adaptation, and there can be that pulling away that is really difficult."

For some families, Painter says, farming provides a domain of competence for refugee parents or grandparents who rely, often humiliatingly, upon their English-speaking children for help at the doctor's office, the bank, the registry of motor vehicles, or parent-teacher conferences. Gardening, Painter says, "seems to provide something for parents to pass on to their children." Over the years, Painter has noticed "lots of intergenerational interactions . . . where you'll see everyone from grandparents to little babies out in the gardens."

Nearly all the refugees who participate in the Global Gardens program enjoyed long farming traditions in their countries of origin. But when they arrived in the United States, they could not afford to rent or buy homes that had enough land for a garden. Typically, refugees end up in apartment complexes or in lower-cost housing, where at best they would have room to plant some flowers or grow a few tomato plants in pots. While working with refugees in the plots provided by Global Gardens, Painter has talked with dozens of refugees who simply find peace of mind and contentment from the routines and nurturing rituals of growing and harvesting. This has been especially true, she's found, for men and women who came to the United States near or at retirement age.

"Think about the experience of being a refugee. You are leaving behind everything that is familiar. Maybe you've faced trauma, been exposed to terrible violence, lost your loved ones," Painter says. "If you come to the United States from, say, Russia or Burma at sixty or sixty-five, it's going to be challenging to adjust, to find a place in the society. It's not like it is for young people who go to school, who are taught English. Just to have this one, controllable piece of land to take care of, a domain where you decide what to plant, how much to plant, and you are doing something so good for yourself, getting outside, maybe socializing with other folks in the garden. You are doing something positive. For a good share of the people we meet and work with, it's about healing."

Painter and her staff offer regular workshops for the refugee gardeners and farmers. Topics include planning, basic planting, and information about the soil of the western United States, water and irrigation, and how to market products. Meanwhile, volunteer mentors—experienced farmers from this agriculturally rich part of the nation—spend an average of two hours a week helping farmers who are selling their produce or who aspire to make some money from their gardens. Most of the people Painter calls the "market farmers" come from African nations, a large share of them Somali Bantus who began settling in Boise in the mid-2000s. Mentors help the farmers harvest and assist at farmers' markets, especially if farmers' English skills are still developing. Painter and her staff, along with the volunteer mentors, also help farmers understand the orders so they harvest the correct products, and they help the farmers keep track of income and expenses. In 2010, Global Gardens published and started selling a cookbook featuring recipes from Boise's refugees and vivid photos of the contributors. There's a rice-and-beans dish from Burundi, Somali Bantu rice made with cardamom and cumin, and *sirnica*, a cheese pita from Bosnia.

Back at the farmers' market, the news has spread: if you find Safiya Abdi's booth, you can get twenty pounds of the most beautiful, just-picked, incredibly delicious tomatoes ever for just thirty bucks. Katie Painter had posted the alert on Facebook and in a group e-mail message.

"Are you Safiya?" a young woman asks, checking her phone. "I got an e-mail from Katie."

Safiya Abdi, one of Global Gardens' most successful market farmers, smiles widely at her customer.

"I think you are here for some tomatoes. Am I right?"

The customer eyes the tomatoes.

"What? Whoa. Those are like the nicest-looking tomatoes I've seen in a while," she says. "I'm making spaghetti sauce."

Safiya had spent much of the previous day squatting and stooping as she harvested those boxes upon boxes of tomatoes. She also picked squash, eggplants, radishes, green beans, cilantro, and lettuce. As she worked, a Somali recitation of the Quran emanated from her smartphone, which she had tucked into her traditional long African dress. Hoisting a thirty-pound box of tomatoes off the ground, Safiya tilted her head back toward a dozen or so rows of corn.

"See all that there? That's my corn. That's the corn that we like, that I grow for Somali people," she explained. Her corn, Safiya said, is less sweet than the ears of corn sold in the United States. "Your corn! It is okay. But it tastes like candy," she joked. Safiya explained that a common Somali food tradition is to roast, grind, and then sift the corn into meal for *soor,* a staple of Somali cuisine that is similar to polenta or grits.

"People, no matter how happy they are to be in America, they still want food from their culture," Safiya said. "So there is some of it, there in this field. Yes. I think it's very good to have that growing there."

Safiya's mother taught her how to farm soon after the family arrived as refugees in Boise in 2005. Like many Somali Bantus, a marginalized ethnic group in Somalia, Safiya's family had owned land that they farmed near the Jubba River in Somalia. After the start of the brutal civil war that began in 1991, Safiya's family fled over the border to a sprawling refugee camp in Kenya, where there was neither room nor freedom to farm. Using scarce water for farming, Safiya says, "was not possible. Water was to drink."

"I think it helped my mother to come here and to farm here and to teach me," Safiya says now. "I feel so grateful to her for that."

Farming was the domain of the Bantus in Somalia. Farmers had a lower status in Somalia than did the pastoralists, who own and herd livestock. As Safiya says, "Our only opportunities were in the gardens. This was a history that my mother taught me. That the gardens were our life, our survival." In Somalia, traditional gender roles usually consign women to child rearing and homemaking. Nevertheless, Bantu women have a long history as successful farmers, though typically they've worked on land owned and controlled by men. Here in Boise, Safiya named her own small business "Safari Farm." She also works full-time at the deli at a local supermarket.

After her enthusiastic tomato customers leave, Safiya rips a paper towel from a roll and uses it to pick cigarette butts off the ground near her booth. She sees a couple of crushed soda cans just outside her booth. She dashes out in the light rain, picks them up, and tosses them in a recycling bin.

"I like my space to look nice, you know? It is my space and it's my business name on it," Safiya says. "Just like I want the vegetables to look beautiful. I like it all to look nice. I think people like that."

A gray-haired man wearing a black Patagonia jacket and bright blue running shoes glances at Safiya's booth and zips by with a quick, wide stride. A few feet past, he stops abruptly, turns on his heel, and walks back toward her.

"Wait!" he exclaims, pointing to Safiya. "This is Safari Farm! I found you! This is where I got those carrots! It's you! Gosh! I'm getting more carrots. I got some last week."

"Well, I'm so glad that you liked them," Safiya says.

"Oh, sure. I loved them, in fact. They reminded me of back home, when I was a kid. They tasted like the kind we used to grow." The man explains that his grandparents used to grow carrots and other vegetables on a small farm in Twin Falls, Idaho.

Within the national community of people concerned with immigrant and refugee integration, Boise, Idaho, enjoys a reputation as a welcoming, forward-looking city. In recent years, the Idaho Office for Refugees has brought together a variety of nonprofits, social service agencies, and city and school officials to systematically assess refugees' needs in this city of about 214,000 people. The series of discussions and meetings resulted in the Refugee Resource Strategic Community Plan. Officials from the various agencies concerned with refugees set goals in the six focus areas of education, employment, health, housing, social integration, and transportation. Then action steps were assigned in each category to various members of the planning group. (In 2013, the White House honored the Idaho Office for Refugees director Jan Reeves as one of ten "Champions of Change" working to integrate immigrants into the lives of their communities.) Among policy experts and advocates, Boise's plan is widely considered a national model for proactive, effective community planning related to refugees and immigrants.

After planners identified a weak public transportation system as a barrier to refugees getting to jobs, for example, the transportation committee created a program to provide free van rides, not just to refugees but to numerous "dependent populations" such as the elderly. Simultaneously, transportation experts created a job training program to provide refugees jobs as van drivers and in the growing bicycle transportation industry. After human service providers expressed a need for training in refugee-related matters for social workers and other human service providers, educators at Boise State College in 2011 began offering special training leading to three different types of certification in refugee services. The courses are intended both for people currently working in a variety of fields, such as education and health services, that serve refugees and for undergraduates and graduate students.

The Idaho Office for Refugees, working with a variety of agencies, has helped resettle more than nine thousand refugees in and around Boise since 1998. Boise grew into a popular refugee resettlement site after the early 1980s, when refugees came from Vietnam, Laos, and Cambodia. Around the same time, persecuted and marginalized refugees from Czechoslovakia, Hungary, Bulgaria, and Romania, then dominated by the Soviet Union, were settled in the city. Toward the end of that decade, refugees began arriving from the Soviet Union itself, including persecuted Jews, Christians, and political dissidents. Several highly active members of the Solidarity movement in Poland also settled in Boise, along with hundreds of Meskhetian Turks, who during World War II had been persecuted by Soviet officials and deported from their homeland in Georgia. The Meskhetian Turks, who are Muslim, continued to face persecution and violence in Uzbekistan and Russia and other places where they had settled. In the 1990s Idaho officials resettled about 2,500 people fleeing the ethnic cleansing, civil war, and violence of Bosnia and Herzegovina. During that period, another 2,500 people came from African nations, East Asia, Central Asia, and the Caribbean. By the early 2000s refugees were continuing to come from Bosnia and Herzegovina, Uzbekistan, Afghanistan, and Russia. Refugees from several African nations, including Somalia, Sudan, and Liberia, also settled in Boise. Midway through the decade, more African refugees arrived, including more people from Somalia, the Congo, and Sudan, along with people from Togo, Ethiopia, and other nations.

"The planning that we finally took on to assist refugees, to draw attention to those needs, was accomplished in the depths of the recession. That downturn helped inspire the work. What's hopeful, to me, is that we never heard that kind of resentment you often get in communities when resources are getting scarce," Reeves says. "You certainly had folks saying we need more resources to help English language learners, to help get people toward self-sufficiency. You heard people talking about this in terms of a challenge they were facing. But it was all done in the spirit of serving members of the community, of wanting to do more, of figuring out how to do things better."

In such a heavily white state and city, many refugees are, Reeves says, "pretty visible," adding, "And I think that visibility is a good thing. Conversations start. People ask questions. A lot of people here may not have much experience with diversity, given our demographics. But there also tends to be a pretty good-natured curiosity among people." Programs like Global Gardens, which try to engage refugees with the larger community "increases that visibility . . . that awareness that the membership in our community is getting more diverse and that refugees are contributing in very concrete ways." Reeves is inspired, too, about a long vacant strip mall in Boise recently developed as the Boise International Market. The market provides low-overhead booths and space for a variety of small businesses, including restaurants, art, and other goods from all over the world. Many of the vendors are immigrants and refugees.

Part of Boise's image as a welcoming community may stem from its renown and pride as a center for Basque immigration, culture, and history. Basques are likely the oldest ethnic group in Europe, according to Mark Kurlansky, author of the book *A Basque History of the World.* However, Basques have never had their own nation. Informally, Basque country includes seven principal provinces in Western Europe, straddling the Pyrenees Mountains, where Spain and France meet. The Basque language, Kurlansky writes, is similar to no other known language. People began leaving Basque country for the United States in the 1800s. In Idaho, Basques found work as miners and sheepherders. Southern Idaho has one of the largest Basque American populations in the United States, with much of that population—about fifteen thousand people—centered in Boise. Boise's Basque Cultural Center and Museum, several Basque restaurants, historic buildings, and a community center make up the "Basque Block" on Grove Street downtown. An old court used for fronton (a type of handball) has been preserved, as have two former boardinghouses where Basque immigrants once lived. The Basque Community Center offers traditional dance classes for children and adults. Basque Americans often meet there to socialize and play a Basque card game called *mus.*

Boise's mayor, David Bieter, elected to three consecutive terms since 2003, is a third-generation Basque American. Since his election in 2003 Bieter, a local son, has set a tone of inclusion in his speeches and public comments. He often emphasizes the benefits of diversity in a state where 94 percent of the population is white. (Nationally, white people are about 78 percent of the population.) In deeply red Idaho, Bieter, a Democrat, has frequently praised Boise's "caring qualities" with regard to refugees. He's been a vocal supporter of gay marriage and was the first mayor in Idaho to sign the U.S. Mayors Climate Protection Agreement, which commits the city to reducing greenhouse gases. Bieter also oversaw the preservation of a twenty-six-mile greenbelt on either side of the Boise River, which runs through the city.

A few miles from the Basque Block, Global Gardens' Jordan Street Garden sits on a corner in a quiet family neighborhood of modest, well-kept single-family homes. With small grants and donations, members of the local neighborhood association founded this garden in 2009 after the landowner donated the vacant lot. The founders aspired to create a community garden that would provide a space for refugees and other people who live in this predominantly white, middle-class neighborhood to garden together and get to know each other. About fifteen refugee families, many of whom live in the Davis Park Apartments, just down the block, tend plots here. A smaller community garden sits adjacent to the Global Gardens plots. The refugee farmers have remarkably diverse origins—Bhutan, Syria, Bosnia, Somalia, the Democratic Republic of the Congo, Russia. Members of the neighborhood association also sponsor potlucks, movie nights, and other celebratory events with the garden as the hub. Jordan Street Garden is also a Global Gardens CSA pickup spot.

One sunny afternoon a woman originally from Bhutan cuts bright red cherry tomatoes in half and spreads them across cardboard to dry them in the afternoon sun. Three seven-year-old boys, who live in the Davis Park apartment complex, ride up on bicycles. They drop their bicycles to the ground and scoot and hop through the garden's stakes, careful not to step on the cabbages, squash, green beans, eggplants, and tomatoes. They happen upon a few shovels leaning against a tree. They begin digging—for no other purpose, it seems, but to dig.

Toward the back of the garden, Lauren Greig sorts bags of basil, lettuce, and boxes of tomatoes for the week's CSA pickup. A transplant from Indiana, Grieg took her beloved job at Global Gardens after an unsatisfying and brief career as a scientist in corporate agribusiness. A botanist by training, Greig provides technical assistance to refugee farmers and helps coordinate the CSA pickups. She brings tables out to the street, covers them with African-print cloths, and arranges the food in straw baskets. Today's CSA share—costing about $20 a week—includes five pounds of tomatoes, two small eggplants or one large one, the choice of basil or cilantro, a bunch of carrots, a choice of a one-pound bag of greens (lettuce, arugula, or spinach), and a huge chunk of banana squash, which looks like the better-known butternut but, Lauren says, "is supposedly meatier, though I think that 'meaty' is a weird word to use for a squash."

Just after two o'clock, customers begin to arrive in a steady stream. Fit-looking white women, some in professional work clothes, others in workout gear or jeans, and a few young couples pull up in Subarus, minivans, and small SUVs. There are lots of toddlers and school-age children in tow.

Julia Grant and her four-year-old son, Theo, drive up to the Jordan Street CSA pickup station not long after taking a seven-mile hike in the foothills that surround the city.

"We are trying to get to five pounds of tomatoes," Julia tells Theo. "Can you do that? Can you weigh the tomatoes?" Theo considers his task intently, his eyes moving between the overflowing box of tomatoes and the scale on the table. Gingerly he starts placing tomatoes on the scale.

With four children between the ages of four and eleven, a love for fresh fruits and vegetables, but hardly any land at their home in Boise's North End, Grant and her husband have long been "faithful and enthusiastic" customers of community-supported agriculture programs in and around the city.

Later that night, the gardeners and neighbors at Jordan Street block off traffic and gather for a potluck featuring fresh food from the garden, a bike parade for the kids, and a screening of the children's movie *The Goonies*. A photo album chronicling the garden's evolution sits open on a table festooned with balloons. A sign announces volunteer opportunities: fall tilling, manure spreading, and "any ideas for projects to make the garden more welcoming, beautiful, productive and safe!" Children run, scoot, pedal bikes and tricycles, chase one another, and play in the dirt. Lawn chairs line both sides of the street. The potluck offerings include gluten-free and dairy-free pumpkin chocolate bars, unadorned freshly picked green beans, noodle kugel, lots of salads, and *seviyaan*, a noodle-based dish popular in Southeast Asia.

Sitting on a lawn chair and wearing a wide smile, Zamira Abdullayera stares at the Jordan Street garden. Her grandson sits on her lap munching on nacho cheese chips and cherry tomatoes. Abdullayera was one of the first refugees to begin gardening at Jordan Street, a few years after she moved into an apartment in Boise.

"When I lived in Russia, I had a beautiful garden. Oh, I grew everything. We had green beans, tomatoes, cucumbers, all the veggies. We moved here and there was no room for a garden. It just was not possible. And this made me sad. I missed it very much," she says. Out for a walk one afternoon in 2008, Abdullayera saw "people doing things with shovels and dirt, and I knew what was happening. They were creating a garden! I was so happy."

Now she teaches her grandson to plant and nurture flowers, cucumbers, peppers, tomatoes, and most recently raspberries.

"I planted those just to try it. One little bush of raspberries," she says. "And now they are everywhere. I see people finding them and eating them, and when I see that it makes me feel good. I started that."

Pretty much everyone at the potluck celebration enthusiastically tries each other's food contributions. They offer one another praise, frequently via the internationally recognized thumbs-up sign. But in spite of all the trying, barriers to verbal communication between the adult nonrefugees and most of their refugee neighbors remain pretty high, at least tonight. With some exceptions, members of the various ethnic groups—this of course includes the white, English-speaking people—tend to stick together. It is an altogether different matter for the children, however, who all run and play in a diverse, jubilant, largely English-speaking pack. And the grown-ups do take responsibility for other people's kids, in spite of language barriers. They pick up and brush off kids who fall off their bikes. They help disoriented toddlers find their parents. They slice up pears and hand them out. Once in a while, children of refugees help interpret for their parents so the grown-ups can talk with each other.

First grader Junior Merciel, sweaty and a bit breathless after racing his bike up and down the street, says he "loves" the Jordan Street Garden.

"It's just a really good-feeling place! Look around at us!" says Junior, whose parents moved to Idaho from the Democratic Republic of the Congo several years ago. Junior sweeps his arm across the scene.

"I would just say that we are probably the happiest kids in the entire world," he declares. With that, Junior pedals feverishly back to his friends.

OMAHA, NE

Omaha ★

PRECISELY THIS PATCH OF EARTH

In America's Heartland, Three Faiths Share
Space, Build Relationships, and Create
an International Model of Pluralism

Augusta National in Georgia. Shoal Creek near Birmingham. Cypress Point in Monterey, California. Oakland Hills in suburban Detroit. Caldwell in Louisiana. The Los Angeles Country Club. These are just several of the many country clubs in the United States that only a generation or two ago barred Jews, African Americans, and people of other minority religions, races, and ethnicities from membership. In 1962, the Anti-Defamation League of B'nai B'rith inspected 803 country clubs and found that more than 70 percent of clubs practiced some form of racial, cultural, or religious discrimination.

Rt. Rev. Scott Barker, who in 2011 became bishop of the Episcopal Diocese of Nebraska, grew up in Omaha and attended exactly those sorts of clubs, to which his parents and grandparents belonged. In those days, the clubs the Barkers enjoyed would not have admitted a guy like Bob Freeman, a local

Jewish business and real estate lawyer whose family has lived in Omaha for four generations.

"The country clubs . . . were completely segregated both racially and in terms of religion," recalls Barker, who is in his early fifties. "My family was complicit in all that."

Omaha's Jewish community, meanwhile, had built their own leisure facility in 1924—the Highland Country Club, at 132nd Street and Pacific Street in west Omaha.

"When the Jews in Omaha, and probably many other cities in the U.S., were originally denied access to local country clubs, they needed a place to socialize and play golf, so they built clubs for themselves," explains Freeman, who is in his early sixties. His maternal grandparents belonged to Highland. "As we often see," Freeman says, "an initial exclusion forces a group to become even more insular."

By the late 1980s, most of Omaha's country clubs had dropped their barriers. The famous investor and Omaha son Warren Buffett, one of the world's wealthiest people, who is not Jewish, joined Highland in the mid-1980s. Country club competition in golf-happy Omaha was tough, however, and in an effort to attract new members, Highland in 1999 took out a $10.7 million loan to make improvements. It renamed itself Ironwood Country Club. But new members never materialized and the club went bankrupt a decade later.

Highland's demise, however, didn't end Freeman's connection to the land. At the time of the bankruptcy Freeman was a board member of Temple Israel, Omaha's Reform Jewish congregation. He was working closely with Dr. Syed Mohiuddin, a Muslim and a prominent cardiologist at Creighton University, and with Reverend Tim Anderson, an Episcopal priest, on something called the Tri-Faith Initiative. The initiative members aspired to build a synagogue, mosque, and church on common property in an unprecedented experiment in interfaith coexistence. Since 2006, the year the Tri-Faith Initiative idea was conceived, the men had considered at least five or six sites that could have potentially accommodated three houses of worship, a fourth shared building for interfaith celebrations and community meetings, plus a parking lot. Nothing had ever panned out.

Motivated by the vision of bringing together Jews, Muslims, and Christians at a time when religious strife roils America and much of the world, the men kept looking. When the 153-acre former Highland Country Club went up for auction in 2010, Tri-Faith sent a representative over. And in 2011, the three faith communities finalized a deal for four parcels of land spanning thirty-five acres, at about $170,000 per acre. Within months, the former golf course, once an outgrowth of segregation, was being transformed into what is perhaps the most innovative and most purposeful attempt at collaborative interfaith living in the world.

"The four structures are an icon," says the Episcopal priest, Tim Anderson. "This is what we should be able to do. We want to be an example of what can be done."

In the summer of 1975, a tornado ripped through central Omaha. It destroyed homes and at Temple Israel, on Cass Street, shattered several stained-glass windows that commemorated *ner tamid*, or "eternal light." Temple members collected hundreds of giant glass shards and meticulously restored the windows. Those restored stained-glass windows are part of the new synagogue being built on the Tri-Faith site.

"There's no way we could have left those behind—they have an immense amount of meaning," says John Waldbaum, the commercial real estate financier who represented Tri-Faith at the auction of Highland. Like a lot of Jewish kids at the time, Waldbaum had celebrated his bar mitzvah at Highland, where his family belonged.

A temple, Waldbaum says, requires three components: worship, community, and education. Accordingly, the 59,000-square-foot temple's sanctuary accommodates about 800 people. A circular chapel holds another 125. There are offices for the rabbi, the cantor, and other temple officials, classrooms, and a large social hall with floor-to-ceiling windows and a terrace that looks across gently sloping hills to where organizers expect a mosque and a church to sit by 2016.

The final building, the shared Tri-Faith Center, will host films, lectures, and other common events, and include conference rooms and a café where people from a variety of faiths can mingle. That building has been designed to resemble a tent like that of Abraham, to whom all three faiths trace their roots. Abraham's tent was kept open on all four sides as a sign of welcome to travelers approaching from any direction. And, in a humorous coincidence, the property is bisected by Hell Creek; it is now traversable via the new Heaven's Bridge. (The former country club property, renamed Sterling Ridge, will include residential housing, a senior center, and office buildings, in addition to the Tri-Faith campus.)

It may surprise some people that this is happening in Nebraska, which is not widely perceived as a bastion of multiculturalism. But Omaha's past suggests the Tri-Faith project may not be so out of place. Founded in the mid-1850s, Omaha's first settlers included many Jews, eleven of whom founded Temple Israel in 1871. When U.S. troops arrested Chief Standing Bear of the Ponca tribe and detained him at Fort Omaha in 1879 for the crime of leaving his reservation, Christian and Jewish clergymen came together to write angry letters to federal government officials demanding his release. Two prominent local attorneys sued the U.S. government for Standing Bear's right to be treated as an equal human being, arguing that he had as much right to move around the country as anybody else in the United States. They won.

In 1977, a historically white Episcopal congregation in north Omaha and a historically black one began sharing Lenten services. About a decade later, in 1986, the two congregations merged and became the Episcopal Church of the Resurrection. According to church officials, it is the only parish in the state that is "fully integrated by black and white Episcopalians." Another congregation in north Omaha, New Life Presbyterian, also merged two previously separate churches, one white and one black. Omaha, though, was also the setting for the Academy Award–nominated 1967 documentary *A Time for Burning*, about a white Lutheran minister's attempts to reach out to African American neighbors. The film exposed virulent racism within the white community and within religious groups, and it ignited a long-lasting controversy in a changing city.

There is plenty of room for integration in this extremely segregated region, but greater Omaha is certainly more diverse now than it was in the days when Barker and Freeman were growing up. (Freeman and Barker's daughters, Freeman says, were "best pals" in elementary school.) Omaha has attracted immigrants since its founding in the mid-1800s. South Omaha was usually the first stop for Omaha's immigrants, which included Poles, Czechs, Irish, and Germans, who for generations attended separate Catholic churches. Over the decades, those immigrant groups tended to move out of working-class south Omaha either to west Omaha or to the rapidly developing suburbs. Latinos, beginning with Mexican Americans, have a long history in Omaha, having first arrived in significant numbers in the 1860s for jobs in the slaughterhouses of south Omaha and on the railroads. (Union Pacific, still headquartered in Omaha, had built the first transcontinental railroad in the 1860s.) Latinos remain concentrated and well established in south Omaha, where independent small businesses, churches, and the popular art and history museum El Museo Latino are community anchors.

Between 2000 and 2010, immigration increased by 56 percent in Nebraska, which is double the national rate. Latinos are Omaha's fastest-growing immigrant group and have an increasing presence in Nebraska's more rural areas, too. Traditionally Catholic, Latinos have in recent years been moving into the Episcopalian faith. Omaha, because of active Catholic Charities and Lutheran Church agencies, is also a long-standing active area of resettlement for refugees from many nations, including South Sudan and since the 2000s, Somalia, a Muslim nation. Swahili is one of the most common of the more than one hundred different languages Omaha Public Schools students speak. Between 2000 and 2010, the Latino population in Nebraska increased by 77 percent, and Latinos now make up 9 percent of the state's population. The Asian population, meanwhile, while still just 2 percent of the state population, increased by 47 percent during the decade. Immigration alone certainly didn't spur the faith-based effort, but Tri-Faith organizers agree that the growing cultural and religious diversity in the region makes interfaith and intercultural efforts not only more feasible but more urgent. This becomes especially clear when looking at projections indicating that the racial and cultural and, thus, religious makeup of the entire state will grow markedly more diverse in the coming years. People of color will make up about 33 percent of Nebraska's population by 2040, according to census projections.

"I love telling people that 30 percent of Nebraska's children under the age of five are Latino," says Ted Stillwill, CEO of the Omaha-based Learning Community, which develops and oversees educational programs in the region. "I love saying that because people just don't believe it and it makes them pay attention. . . . People have their image and their stereotypes about Nebraska, that it's cornfields and white people. But of course the data is right there. It tells the story about the fact that we are changing, that we really need to provide ways for all children to prepare for that diverse world, to be part of that world."

From 2000 to 2010, the Omaha region's Muslim population increased by 187 percent, according to the Association of Religion Data Archives (ARDA). This represented the region's second-fastest-growing religious group, after the Pentecostal Church of God Prophecy, which, according to ARDA, has only about 140 adherents. That said, Omaha's Muslim community is still relatively small, with about 4,600 adherents, compared to, for example, nearly 190,000 Catholics and 105,000 evangelical Protestants, according to ARDA.

"This idea of interfaith cooperation goes to the earliest days of Omaha," says Nancy Kirk, an Episcopalian who has been Tri-Faith's executive director since 2008. But for all its ambition, the Tri-Faith idea was born in part from practicality. Temple Israel used to sit next to Omaha's Community Playhouse, where Henry Fonda and Marlon Brando once performed, and across the street from the First United Methodist Church, a quiet and respectful neighbor. And because their schedules were so different, they could use one another's parking lots on overflow days. But Temple Israel's Cass Street synagogue had been built in 1954 for just 300 families. By the early 2000s, some 750 families were worshipping there. It suffered from a leaky roof and other structural maladies. The temple soon had an opportunity to build on a thirty-acre piece of land, but the site was too large for their needs. Freeman wondered if they might be able to find partners to share the land. Freeman suggested the idea of shared space to Temple Israel's rabbi, Aryeh Azriel. The rabbi immediately knew whom he wanted to be his neighbor.

Aryeh Azriel was born in Israel in 1950, two years after his parents emigrated from Sofia, Bulgaria. His parents were respectful of major Jewish holidays, but there was no ritualistic life. His bar mitzvah, for example, had no religious component to it, but was "just a party." Polio left him with a serious limp, but Azriel was an active kid. The summer after his last year in high school, in 1967, he traveled with several friends to work at a Reform Jewish summer camp in Wisconsin, and then traveled through the United States with them. The camp proved illuminating for Azriel, who had always been curious about the spiritual side of his Jewish identity.

"I was able to talk to liberal rabbis, and I was shocked, in a good way, to hear what they had to say about religion," he says. Azriel. "I found God in America. I saw what the theology of Judaism was all about."

Azriel and his friends returned to Israel and planned to reunite to look at slides from their trip. But their plans were dashed when the Six-Day War started a few days later. By the time the war had ended, two of his friends were dead.

"Why is this project so important to me? It has to do with the pain of growing up in Israel and the Middle East, and not being able to contribute to a process of peace," he says. "Their death and the wars still affect me today. This has been one of the ways of restoring the souls of my friends." After time in Israel and Chicago, Azriel attended Hebrew Union College in Cincinnati. Following his graduation in 1983, he became an assistant rabbi in Baltimore. Seeing that Azriel was hungry for greater responsibility, the head rabbi encouraged him to seek a chief rabbi's position, which, in 1988, led him to Temple Israel in Omaha. He was impressed by what he found in Nebraska.

"People were generous, and they really celebrated their identities," Ariel says. "The midwestern values are important. People still know how to be kind to each other here." Even before he arrived for his job interview, Azriel noted, the congregation had built a railing to the pulpit that would help him, with his limp, get up the steps. He also liked that the community had a long history of interfaith activity and opened its services to everyone. "Almost every Friday and Saturday there is a group of visitors here," Azriel says proudly.

He also forged ties with Omaha's Muslims. After 9/11 someone threatened to torch the Islamic Center of Omaha. Azriel led several Jews to the mosque, where they stood guard. And so it would make sense that Rabbi Azriel loves Bob Freeman's idea about choosing partners to share land. He told Freeman that the Jewish temple's new neighbors should be the Muslims he had gotten to know.

Syed Mohiuddin was born in 1934 in the city of Hyderabad in southeastern India to a strict Muslim family that, through his mother's side, could trace its roots to Syed Abdel Qadir Gilani

Al Amoli, a twelfth-century preacher who founded the Qa-
diri Sufi order of Islam. Relations between Hyderabad's majority Hindus and minority Muslims were generally good, so
when Mohiuddin came to Omaha for his residency at Creighton University Medical Center in 1963, he was accustomed to a
life of peaceful coexistence as a religious minority. After taking
a teaching job in 1970 at Creighton, Mohiuddin climbed the
ranks and in 2007 became chair of the Department of Medicine. Spending his entire medical career at Creighton, which
is a Jesuit institution, exposed Mohiuddin to Catholicism and
gave him the opportunity to introduce his faith to Catholics. "I
learned a lot about Catholicism, and people would also ask me
questions about Islam," he recalls. Mohiuddin had less experience with Jews, but a mutual acquaintance of his and Rabbi
Azriel's suggested to the rabbi that he contact Mohiuddin about
the interfaith idea.

At the time, Mohiuddin and a small group of Muslim professionals had wanted to start a new Islamic center in Omaha that
would be both a place of worship and an educational center that
could host discussions and cultural events exploring Islam's various interpretations and practices in the United States and around
the world. Mohiuddin and his colleagues knew that many Americans had negative views of Islam, and despite always having felt
at home in Omaha, he still occasionally would hear random remarks equating Muslims with terrorism. "Which is still very
painful to me, because that's not the way I know Islam," he says.
"For many Americans, what they know about Islam comes from
what they see on the news, from all the things happening over-
seas. People needed to get to know Islam in this country."

So when Rabbi Azriel and a small group of Jews presented
the idea to Mohiuddin and a few Muslims at a meeting at local
public library in January 2006, the Muslims saw it as the perfect
opportunity for the Islamic center.

"When the invitation came, we thought it would be wonderful," Mohiuddin says. "Whenever Muslims participate in

interfaith events and talk with people of other faiths, the results are almost always positive." The American Institute of Islamic Studies and Culture (AIISC) was incorporated later that year. Run out of a small office complex in west Omaha, it hosts Friday prayers, meetings, and other events. Its mission is to "promote a better understanding of Islam in the Western world," and its vision is to "create an institution which will affirm the core values of Islam, which are: Acceptance, Compassion, Equality, Justice, and Peace."

"We've always been on the defensive," says Karim Khayati, who emigrated from Tunisia to Nebraska in 1998 and is one of Tri-Faith's newer board members. "Here we're not on the defensive. We're taking part in something big, something that's sending a positive message."

The next step was to reach out to a Christian congregation, and the most obvious choice seemed to be the Catholic Church, the largest Christian denomination in Omaha (and in the United States). But the Omaha archdiocese was about $8 million in debt. Its membership was in decline, leaving leaders in no position to finance a new church. Tri-Faith organizers also considered the Lutheran and Methodist churches, but leaders of those faiths faced similar financial uncertainties. Freeman then thought of the denomination his wife, Robyn, belonged to: the Episcopal Church. At the time, Rev. Tim Anderson was just about two years into his job as assistant to the bishop of the Episcopal diocese of Nebraska, Rt. Rev. Joe Burnett, who had tasked Anderson with developing congregations. Burnett, Anderson recalled, told him a bit about the interfaith effort, saying, "I don't know what this is about, but check it out."

It was an unusual assignment for Anderson, who was born and raised in Kearney, a small city in central Nebraska where, as far as he knew, there was only one Jewish family.

"I didn't come from a diverse background. It was pretty

vanilla," he says, just before taking part in a Sunday evening service at St. Augustine of Canterbury Episcopal Church in Elkhorn, a neighborhood on Omaha's western edge. But Anderson did have what he calls the gift of hospitality, which first took him into the restaurant business and later, in 1981, to seminary. "That gift serves me well. I'm very open to others," says Anderson, whose first parish assignments were in the small cities of Blair and Grand Island, Nebraska, the latter of which has experienced a sharp increase in its Latino population in recent years. In 2003, he was one of the delegates at the Episcopalian national convention who voted in favor of consecrating as a bishop Rev. Gene Robinson, who is gay and in a same-sex marriage. In 2004, the church posted Anderson to Omaha. The same way some people may look for a home steps away from the beach or a subway stop, Anderson, an avid golfer, found a home steps away from the Iron Horse Golf Club in Ashland, about twenty-seven miles southwest of Omaha.

When Anderson first called Freeman to talk, he was told he would have to try later, after Freeman returned from a golfing trip in Scotland. "To me that was a good sign. Golf is one of my passions," Anderson says. When Freeman returned, in August 2006, he drove to meet Anderson at the Iron Horse Golf Club, where he planned to pitch the Tri-Faith idea to him. "By the third hole we were so excited we didn't care about the game," Anderson recalled. For him, the Tri-Faith project would mark the start of a personal journey. The project also corresponded with plans the Episcopal Diocese of Nebraska had to build a new congregation and church. Sharing a parking lot with two other faith groups appealed to Episcopal leaders' sense of thrift and ecumenism.

"After 9/11 I saw this as an opportunity to do something very unique, and not just benefit our three groups, but all of Omaha," says Anderson, who had not even met any Muslims until 2006, through his involvement in Tri-Faith. Anderson established a quick connection with Muslim community members based on what he called a "mutual desire to serve the community."

"I've passed out dates during Ramadan, and I've been at temple when the little ones are given the scrolls," Anderson says. "Those are experiences with those faith groups that I will always cherish."

Once the three pieces had been put in place, the people involved decided that in order to maintain momentum, they would have to skip a honeymoon period and immediately address a hodge-podge of fears and difficult questions: How ambitious should the project be? Who would own the buildings? How would they govern relations between the communities and handle disagreements between them? What if people start trying to convert each other? In response to these worries the faith leaders wrote a memorandum of understanding in November 2006. It affirmed each group's independence to control its buildings and run its religious affairs, prohibited proselytizing, and stipulated that participants would "completely respect the beliefs and practices" of the other participants.

Tri-Faith leaders also sought ways to build bridges between their followers. They created a series of classes called Tri-Faith 101, where participating Jews, Muslims, and Christians would be introduced to each other's faiths, concentrating in particular upon their commonalities. They have already hosted several interfaith picnics and dinners, including the Abraham's Tent fund-raiser in 2009 that drew eleven hundred people, including national leaders of all three faiths.

In one of the first Tri-Faith activities, parents created a kids' group called Interplay, which meets at least once a month. Children do take part in interfaith-themed games and projects, but mostly they just play together. Meanwhile, parents visit with each other and learn about each other's faith traditions. In August, an interfaith picnic brought out more than four hundred people to the Tri-Faith Campus for halal hamburgers, kosher hot dogs, and a seventy-two-foot-long table full of potluck dishes. Then in October, the kids from the Interplay group learned about Sukkot, the Jewish celebration that is also known as the Festival of Booths. Sukkot commemorates the forty years during which Jewish people wandered the desert and lived in temporary structures. During the holiday, families typically re-create those temporary structures, where they eat their meals and maybe even sleep. At the Tri-Faith Sukkot celebration, children pieced together graham crackers and colorful candles to make miniature replicas of Sukkot shelters. The following month, people of many different faiths shared dinner at Temple Israel for a "neighbor to neighbor" dinner. The dinner followed several months of smaller interfaith dinners people had hosted in their homes. The dinner at the temple brought together all the people who had gotten together for those smaller, private interfaith meals.

Despite the progress at Tri-Faith, the work is far from complete. Routine financial and logistical challenges abound, as they do with any major construction project. (In 2014, for example, the Episcopalians voiced new concerns about the financial wisdom of staying involved in the project. As of early 2015, officials at the Countryside Community Church, a 1,200-member United Church of Christ congregation, were considering whether to move to the Tri-Faith campus, taking over the Episcopalians' role as the Christian presence at Tri-Faith.) Religious diversity introduces other smaller but important challenges. For example, the earliest conceptions of the project envisioned a central kitchen, but once dietary differences were considered—Muslims didn't drink alcohol, Jews didn't eat shellfish or mix dairy and meat products, only the Christians ate pork—it was clear that each group's building would need its own kitchen.

"Raising money is the hardest part. There will always be roadblocks, but I'm confident our ability to communicate will ensure our success," says Nancy Kirk, the Tri-Faith executive director. When Kirk turned sixty she wrote a plan for the next four decades of her life, which included learning about religious pluralism. Much of the work of negotiating disagreements, logistical conflicts, schedules, and other challenges falls on her. A gregarious woman, she has equipped her cell phone with an Islamic prayer-time reminder and other apps suggesting her interest in many faiths.

While Tri-Faith has broad support from different faith communities, not everyone loves the idea. Rabbi Azriel faced the challenge of convincing a well-established congregation that its brand-new temple would be on a site a stone's throw away from a mosque and a Christian church. Most people support the project, but a few holdouts remain, important donors among them. "We are not going to wait for them," Rabbi Azriel says. "We don't have time."

The Episcopalians and Muslims have the very different challenge of building congregations. While members of their faith communities have been generally supportive, some have raised objections. Fund-raising is a slog, and the congregations are still modest in size. "Some family members are not into it," says David Wright of suburban Gretna, just outside Omaha. Wright had come with his wife, Pam, to the Sunday night service led by Anderson at the St. Augustine of Canterbury Church in Elkhorn. Friday prayers at the American Institute of Islamic Studies and Culture attract about twenty worshippers, although holiday services, which the Muslim group has held at a local hotel, bring in more than a hundred people. In contrast, the Islamic Center of Omaha usually gets about three hundred people for Friday prayers and about three thousand people at its holiday services.

Given the competing pressures, how does the group keep something contentious from sinking the project?

"Yeah, I don't know how we do that, because it's not like we haven't had our conflicts, because we have," says Rev. Ernesto Medina of St. Martha's Episcopal Church in Papillion, Nebraska. Medina, who is of Mexican heritage, first came to

Omaha in 2007 as dean for urban mission at Trinity Cathedral in downtown Omaha, where he served a mainly Latino population. He joined the Tri-Faith board in 2010 and became rector at St. Martha's, a predominantly white congregation, in 2012. Part of the reason conflicts arise, Medina says, is because the governing processes of the three worshipping communities differ so much from one another. For example, in the Episcopal Church, leaders usually have the last say on policy and regulations. Rabbis must answer to a board, and Muslims have an even more horizontal leadership structure. Complicating matters are the myriad cultures involved, from American and Israeli Jews to the dozens of nationalities that make up Omaha's Muslim population.

"The Christians, we're always dealing with the fact that we're the dominant culture in this system, so what does that mean for the use of our voice?" Medina says. "At some point we figure it out."

It can be a learning process. Consider Scott Barker, bishop of Nebraska's Episcopal Diocese, who joined the Tri-Faith board in 2013. Growing up without religious or racial diversity as a child, Barker says, he held his own prejudices, which weren't dislodged until he went to Yale as an undergraduate and then spent a year at Boston University Law School, where in the diverse student population he received "some . . . comeuppance." He recalls one incident when he was with a young woman and made an offensive remark about Jews, and she replied, "You know, I'm a Jew."

"I was just mortified. And it became so quickly clear to me that I had a ton of learning and ton of growing to do," Barker says. "I just grew up, and discovered we had far more in common than differences. . . . Our shared humanity meant that there was always a possibility for connecting meaningfully, even with people who I might have real disagreements with about religion or politics or other things that might divide us."

Sharing a common piece of land has compelled not only

conflict but also cooperation. "The shared piece of turf is having its way of constantly calling us back into relationships and having to deal in innumerable ways with our preferences and our differences and our prejudices. In some ways, the genius of the project is precisely the patch of earth," Barker says. "It's the fact of the physical proximity that makes this thing special. But because we're still in the process of building it and dreaming together what it's going to be, the difficult work of building relationships happens exactly in that crucible, exactly in these complicated decisions about parking lots and drainage and bathrooms."

Another reason Tri-Faith has gotten this far is the strong personal relationships that have formed among the leaders. Earlier this year, Rev. Medina and Rabbi Azriel threw a baby shower for one of their Muslim board members, Nuzhat Mahmood.

"That's what we do. That's what makes this so radically different; we're friends with each other. I was holding Nuzhat's baby the day after he was born," Medina says. "If I have a pastoral challenge, I have no issue calling Rabbi. We trust each other at that level."

Rev. Anderson agrees. "We've been able to build up a level of trust so that we can share things openly," Anderson says. "It's not just 'Muslims' and 'Jews,' but people you care about. We are at that point."

Rev. Barker emphasizes theological aspects. "A thrust of the teaching of Jesus is to love your enemy, pray for those who persecute you. I really believe Christians are called into relationships particularly with people that they might have prejudices toward or have profound disagreements with. . . . As I've matured in my own faith I also have felt more drawn to the challenge of trying to be in a real relationship with people who would be easy to demonize."

Rabbi Azriel thinks the Tri-Faith project is ready for new challenges, like exploring controversial texts from one another's scriptures. Consider the Old Testament story in Genesis of

Abraham, his Hebrew wife, Sarah, and her Egyptian slave girl, Hagar. After failing to conceive a child, Sarah allows Abraham to procreate with Hagar, who gives birth to Ishmael. Sarah grows to hate Hagar and after conceiving her own son, Isaac, commands Abraham to expel Hagar and Ishmael from their tribe into the desert. The Old Testament considers Abraham, Sarah, and Isaac to be the ancestors of Israel and the Jews, while the Quran considers Abraham, Hagar, and Ishmael to be the ancestors of the Arabs, including of Islam's founder, the Prophet Muhammad.

"You can't deal with Muslims and Christians without dealing with the narrative of that story. What do Jewish scholars say about the betrayal of Hagar by Abraham?" asked Azriel. "We may never know the answer, but the issue is that we have to start moving. Every religion has a responsibility to talk about these issues. And if we can move on as a group, that's even better."

Azriel believes it can be done. "I have great hopes. This can be a great place for pilgrims to visit and to see what we've done here, to be inspired, and take that inspiration back to where they came from."

MONTGOMERY
COUNTY, MD

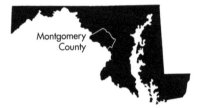

WHY DO WE NEED TO TALK ABOUT RACE SO MUCH?

Montgomery County, Maryland's Educators and Parents Circle In on Culture, Bias, and Learning in Diverse and Changing Schools

Eighteen teachers and administrators sit in a wide circle on fold-out chairs. They've taken a detour from their day jobs at a middle school in Montgomery County, Maryland, to talk about subjects most people try to avoid: race, culture, tension, bias, stereotypes. Some of them do not seem happy to be there.

"I wish we didn't have to have these conversations," a white teacher tells the group. "As a scientist, I see us all as humans."

Her white colleague agrees: "Why do we need to talk about race so much?" she asks.

"I don't want to talk about race either," an African American educator adds. "I wish I could just go home, watch reality TV. I'm not a deep person. I wish I wasn't called names when I was fourteen, but we have kids walking around being diminished."

The African American educator's comments provide one of many reasons the group has gathered. John Landesman, the soft-spoken coordinator who has convened the circle, explains the format—and the goals—for what will be, at times, a testy, touchy two-day session. (Group members asked that their names be withheld so that they would be more comfortable talking freely.)

"We're not speaking about race to be politically correct," Landesman, who is white, tells the group. "We're helping people figure out how to talk to one another. We don't think problems are fixed by going through a study circle."

The teachers and school staff members work at one of an increasing number of public schools where racial and economic demographics have shifted in recent years, in large part due to immigration. As the day wears on, some members of the study circle speak emotionally and with seeming ease about their experiences growing up in countries or cultures different from white, middle-class America. Others, though, continue to question the need to spend a day here, arguing that their time would be better spent back with their students.

Suburban Montgomery County, bordering Washington, D.C., hosts the state's largest public school system. While the county is generally affluent, it is increasingly racially, culturally, linguistically, and economically mixed. The public schools enroll more than 150,000 students in 200 schools across nearly 500 square miles. Students come from more than 157 countries and speak more than 138 languages. Public school officials here have long nurtured and promoted the system's reputation for rigorous academic programs, college-bound high school graduates, and stellar achievement. Over the past decade, students of color have become the majority here, and the share of students from families that earn low incomes has grown. And as is true in so many increasingly diverse suburban districts, the majority of the county's teachers—about 80 percent—are white. (In late 2014, Montgomery school superintendent Joshua Starr announced plans to begin a recruitment effort specifically designed to increase the racial and ethnic diversity of the teaching force.)

* * *

Amid the demographic changes, administrators adopted an ambitious program that starts with a seemingly simple act: people from a variety of racial and cultural backgrounds sit in a circle and talk. The Study Circles Program, started in 2003, organizes and facilitates group conversations at schools for students, parents, and educators, usually with the help of Landesman and his colleagues. Since 2004, the county schools have hosted more than seven hundred study circles. (Circles are convened usually only if staff members have requested the process.) The goals are straightforward: to spur discussion about the ways racial and cultural experiences play out in classrooms, cafeterias, and hallways, how they permeate the learning experience for kids, their effect on teaching practices, and their impact on decision making and policy making among adults. Circle members explore a variety of questions, including: Are students of color treated differently from white students? To what extent is a student's status in school affected by the status of the student's racial or cultural group in the larger society? What are teachers' assumptions about why kids act a certain way or why they do or do not excel? How might adult expectations, unconscious biases, or lack of understanding of students' cultures and experiences set up barriers to students' educational advancement? How might we remove those barriers?

"Ultimately, what I hope is that the status quo isn't OK," says Landesman, the study circles coordinator. The hope, too, is that study circle participants will collaborate on action plans to improve policies and practices or resolve conflicts that they identify together. After developing a shared understanding of a problem, many past and current study circle members do construct these action plans and present their concerns and ideas to school leaders. In recent years, parents and teachers have addressed such challenges as making enrollment in gifted and talented programs better reflect the demographics of a particular school, hiring more bilingual staff members, and training bus drivers who parents had perceived as being disrespectful to students.

About 63 percent of Montgomery County's students are students of color, with Latino students the most numerous (27 percent) of that group. Latino kindergarteners and first graders represent 30.7 percent of students in those grades in Montgomery County, slightly outnumbering white students in those early years. A little more than a third of students come from families with incomes so low they qualify for free and reduced-price school lunch, even though it is still one of the nation's wealthiest counties, with a 2012 median household income of nearly $95,000.

In April, 2014, a report from the Montgomery County Council's Office of Legislative Oversight detailed increasing racial and economic segregation in the county's high schools. The report also noted a widening gap in achievement between white students and students of color. So, even as officials attempt to build relationships and focus on equity on the schools that are becoming more diverse, worsening segregation may very well threaten equity and cross-cultural understanding and interaction in this growing school district. Recent research has indeed shown that socioeconomic integration is strongly associated with improved achievement. In a 2010 study for the RAND Corporation, researcher Heather Schwartz found that students from families earning low incomes who went to schools with lower levels of poverty performed much better over time than their counterparts who attended schools with higher poverty rates, even when per-pupil spending in the higher-poverty schools was $2,000 higher than in the lower-poverty schools, following a deliberate effort to provide more resources to high-poverty schools. Schwartz found that about two-thirds of this effect was due to students having been in a lower-poverty school. The other third of the beneficial effect was due to students living in a lower-poverty neighborhood, via an inclusionary zoning program that encourages construction of affordable housing.

In their 2013 book *Confronting Suburban Poverty in America*, Elizabeth Kneebone and Alan Berube of the Brookings Institution report that during the 2000s more jobs and more people at a variety of income levels moved to Montgomery County. Up until the middle of the decade, the poverty rate dropped slightly. However, Kneebone and Berube find, the Great Recession "more than erased those gains." They find that no other county in the Washington, D.C., region, including the District of Columbia, experienced increases in poverty of the same magnitude during the late 2000s. Specifically, the county lost seven thousand jobs since 2007. The number of residents living below the poverty line surged by two-thirds, with more than thirty thousand people now officially poor.

In 1990, immigrants accounted for fewer than one in five county residents. By 2010, one-third of county residents were immigrants and more than 40 percent of the foreign-born lived in poverty. Nearly all the growth in the county's labor force—96 percent—is attributable to immigrants, according to the state-government-created Maryland Council for New Americans. Jobs created in a booming economy attracted immigrants at both ends of the wealth and education level continuum. As the Maryland Council for New Americans reports, more-educated immigrants, who tend to come from India and other Southeast Asian countries, found work in technology and science industries. Immigrants with less formal education filled numerous lower-wage service-sector jobs in hotels and restaurants, as nannies and landscapers, and in construction. El Salvador, in Central America, is the most common country of origin for immigrants in the county. Immigrants from Vietnam and sub-Saharan Africa have also established identifiable and growing communities in the county.

The signature achievement of former Montgomery County school superintendent Jerry Weast, who hired Landesman to launch the Study Circles Program, was a systemic, very public focus on the disparities in opportunities and achievement between schools in wealthy, largely white "upcounty" communities and poorer, racially mixed "downcounty" communities, such as Silver Spring, which borders Washington, D.C. Weast's efforts are detailed in the book *Leading for Equity: The Pursuit of Excellence in Montgomery County Schools.*

"We have to look at the data and ask ourselves the hard questions," says Tomas Rivera-Figueroa, assistant principal at Parkland Middle School, one of the "downcounty" schools where the leadership team spent two days in a study circle. "Our building has 45 percent Latino [students]," Rivera-Figueroa says. "Why is it that 95 percent have a 2.0 GPA?" And even though 25 percent of the students are African American, "why is it that a majority of suspensions are of African Americans?"

"The kids are the first to say, 'The teacher doesn't understand me,'" says Rivera-Figueroa, who has been Parkland's assistant principal for nine years. "We have to have those conversations and create an understanding."

Parkland offers a textbook case of the changing American suburban school. Its study circle also demonstrates that creating a more inclusive, fair, and successful school will require purposeful, steady work. Students of color—African American, Hispanic, and Asian children—make up 85 percent of the student body. And while the principal is Asian and the assistant principal is Latino, the school staff, by contrast, is nearly 70 percent white. A 2008 report from the Civil Rights Project at UCLA reveals that African American and Latino teachers were far more likely than white teachers to report that they had "quite a bit" or "a great deal" of training in methods designed for racially and culturally diverse classrooms. Specifically, 60 percent of Latino teachers, 58 percent of black teachers, and 70 percent of mixed-race teachers reported these amounts of training, compared with only 42 percent of white teachers, according to the study.

Social psychologists Linda Tropp and Thomas Pettigrew have long explored effective strategies for engendering positive intergroup relationships and reducing prejudice within schools. Recently Tropp and Pettigrew considered findings from studies conducted over six decades with more than a quarter of a million participants in thirty-eight countries. In this meta-analysis, they found that while intergroup face-to-face contact does reduce prejudice, the quality of that contact matters. The more able educators and others are to cultivate meaningful relationships across groups, the more likely that contact will reduce prejudice. As for schools, Tropp and Pettigrew point to the importance of creating opportunities for students to cooperate across racial and ethnic groups. Study circles coordinator John Landesman and other educators in Montgomery County view study circles as a pathway for cultivating these important relationships and for spurring necessary collaboration and cooperation in reaching a shared goal.

Leyla Fandey, Parkland's media specialist, has been an educator for two decades. She seems comfortable speaking in the study circle, telling her peers about her unusual upbringing in Iran, fleeing with her family as a teenager to Germany, then to Germantown, a Montgomery County suburb. She believes strongly, she says, in the need to better understand and affirm students from cultures that are very different from those of most of Montgomery County's teachers. "Our experiences do affect how we teach," she tells her peers sitting with her in the study circle. "When I see immigrant students, I know what they're going through," Fandey tells the group. "Some of them have to be the adults in the home. When I was fifteen, I had to learn German. I remember feeling nauseous: What if I got the translation wrong for my parents?"

The group participates in an exercise debunking stereotypes. Landesman asks each educator to write down three characteristics of his or her culture and three words describing how others might generalize his or her ethnicity. One entry from a member of the circle who is Latino listed as characteristics "proud, family-oriented, throw big parties," and then added for how others might stereotype Latinos "cheap, illegal, uneducated." "What are stereotypes for whites?" Landesman asks the group. "Do we think of stereotypes as nonwhite?" Some of the white educators in the room struggle to characterize their cultures or even list stereotypes they imagine people might have of them: "Christian, white," writes one. "Overprivileged, redneck, racist," writes another. A white teacher comments that she doesn't "look at" race or consider it.

"I think about it every single day," Tomas Rivera-Figueroa, the assistant principal, quickly answers.

The county's longtime fair housing manager and education ombudsman, Ruby Rubens, who is African American, helped start the Study Circles Program with Landesman. At the time, more immigrants from Latin America, Africa, and Asia were moving into what had historically been a predominantly white, prosperous county. Study circles were not inspired by a crisis or a dramatic racially charged incident but represented a proactive measure to prevent hostility and ensure inclusivity during a period of rapid growth and transformative demographic change.

"There had never been a time," Rubens explains, "when that kind of dialogue within a diverse community could take place, and the study circle process was the perfect vehicle."

That process worked well for parent Gladis Calderon, who immigrated to Montgomery County from Guatemala in 1982. A decade ago she was volunteering at her children's elementary school, making copies, running errands for classroom teachers, and attending Parent-Teacher Association meetings. She kept quiet, she says, because at that time her English skills weren't strong, though her desire to be involved in her children's education was.

"I didn't understand what was being said a lot, but my presence helped," she says. Then the school principal asked Calderon to participate in one of the first study circles. "When I was on the PTA, I was the only Latina, I felt left out. The study circles made a big difference. We learned where we all came from, how to help each other out. That made a big difference for me. I had more confidence in myself."

Calderon recruited other Latino parents to participate and volunteer at the school. She joined AmeriCorps, the national volunteer program that provides the Study Circles Program with interns. Upon finishing a three-year program with Ameri-Corps, Calderon accepted a paid position as an outreach coordinator for Study Circles. "The study circles changed my life in many ways," says Calderon, whose older two children are now in college. Her youngest is a high school senior. "I learned to understand other people. I learned that people are shy because they don't know how to have a relationship."

At the newly renovated Redland Middle School in suburban Rockville, a large, middle-class community bordering wealthier Potomac, the Latino population has increased rapidly over the past decade. At Redland, students of color now outnumber white students two to one—a complete flip of demographics from just five years ago. Administrators hosted three study circles at Redland early in the 2013 school year. Organizers convened the first for students who are still learning English. Another circle included the same students and members of the school staff. The third circle brought together Latino parents and staff and administrators. The study circles that included Latino parents were conducted in Spanish with English interpretation provided via headphones that the educators wore. Usually study circles bring together between fifteen and twenty people. But this particular circle attracted more than twenty-five parents, teachers, and staff members. Group members brought food to share: empanadas, pupusas, pizza, and donuts. Mothers and fathers shared stories about education in their native Spanish-speaking countries, where parents were not encouraged to participate and a teacher's word was never questioned. Group members mapped out goals and agreed to form a Latino parent group to fulfill one mission of the study circles: involving parents in identifying needs and helping to shape programming and practice at the schools. The group elected a parent president and vice president, who have since continued to meet. The group now works with school-based staff to make sure paperwork from school is translated into Spanish and that school activities are inclusive of all cultures. For example, sixth graders at all county schools spend two nights at a nature center where they get acquainted with each other. Historically, Latino parents have tended to keep their children at home, which meant their kids missed out on an event designed to build community among class members. Redland's assistant principal, Everett Davis, a graduate of the county's schools, is one of the few bilingual administrators at Redland. He sensed that Latino parents needed to hear not from him but from other Latino parents about the benefits of the school-sponsored trip and about the supervision that the adults provide to the children. After he enlisted Latino volunteers to speak with Latino parents about the excursion, enrollment for the trip spiked.

Back in 2007, Latino parents, most of them from El Salvador, joined with the principal and several teachers at Cannon Road Elementary School in diverse Silver Spring to talk about ways the school could better serve its growing Latino community. As a result of regular study circle meetings, a teacher began offering regular free English classes for parents. Parents coordinated a Spanish-language phone tree to fill each other in on school events, policy changes, and concerns. The group established a schedule for bilingual parents to volunteer at the school to assist parents who did not speak English. The Spanish phone tree let parents know when they can go to the school and get their questions answered.

Back at Parkland Middle School, Leyla Fandey, the Iranian-born media specialist, says she is glad to have participated in a process that was not always easy. She's been at Parkland for about a year, she says, and the study circle helped her get to know her colleagues better and triggered important discussions that need to continue.

"But it was a little bit tense," Fandey says. "Then again, nothing is going to happen unless there is a little tension."

—DALTON, GA—

LIFELINES IN TOUGH TIMES

In a Small Georgia City, Health Care Providers Respond to a Demographic Transformation and Create a Vital Community of Support

Inside the cramped living room of his trailer home in Dalton, Georgia, Juan Cabrera opens a plastic shopping bag holding an intimidating inventory of pills and liquid medicine doctors had prescribed for his failing liver, diabetes, and aching back. A life-size painted image of Jesus Christ stares down at Cabrera, his wife, Estela, and three other women whom this fifty-five-year-old former carpet mill worker has come to view as modern-day saviors.

Esther Familia-Cabrera, Cristina Valdovinos, and Marisol Torres sit on a ragged couch with Juan and Estela. A small television plays at low volume. A fan whirs, providing little respite from Georgia's heat. Outside, Cabrera's five children sit and talk in the trailer's shade. It is nearly a hundred degrees and too hot to play. The three women, trained *promotoras de salud*, take turns picking up each bottle, reading its label, and placing it down to form a neat row. Looking on nervously, Juan's wife, Estela, runs her hand over her sweaty forehead and through her hair. Familia-Cabrera (no relation to Juan Cabrera) sees something disturbing and familiar: Juan has not been taking his medication consistently. Many poorer immigrants like him, the promotoras say, commonly scrimp on their pills. They might take half doses or skip daily regimens altogether to make the supply last longer.

"You have to take them all, you have refills," Familia-Cabrera tells Cabrera in Spanish. "We are here for you, and you know that things will be all right, but you have to follow the instructions. And we'll go over them again with you."

"I was doing better . . . I will take them," he promises Familia-Cabrera.

Valdovinos and Torres review the required dosages with Juan and Estela. Then they draw up a schedule for Cabrera's medication regimen. Valdovinos notices that Cabrera's right lower leg is discolored. There's a dark bruise on his shin. This could be a sign that Cabrera's liver problems are getting worse.

"You have to go see a doctor right away," Valdovinos tells Cabrera.

"I will," he assures her again.

The promotoras talk for a while and then agree on an action plan. They will call Cabrera's doctor and get him in there as soon as possible. They will drive him if he needs a ride. Soon after that consultation, the promotoras will return to the trailer park to check in on Juan and Estela. For Juan Cabrera, a native of Guanajuato, Mexico, the promotoras, some of whom are immigrants themselves, have become lifelines.

The promotoras first met Cabrera after he had been referred by health workers at a local free clinic. His stomach was bloated from a failing liver. He was pale. His illnesses had left him disabled. He was too exhausted and in too much pain to return to work at the recycling department in one of the once prosperous mills that earned Dalton the moniker "Carpet Capital of the World." The worn, unkempt trailer park where Cabrera lives among about 150 other families is known around Dalton as "Mexico Chiquito" or "Little Mexico." In the city's northeast corner, Mexico Chiquito is home mainly to Dalton's newest immigrants and to those who, for a variety of reasons, have not moved far from the bottom of the economic ladder. For some of Dalton's Latinos, the Little Mexico nickname is an insult. The nickname seems to imply that Mexico, a vibrant, diverse nation with a proud history and long traditions, is somehow comparable to this collection of insubstantial trailers with broken windows and discarded tires dotting the landscape. Alas, the name stuck. Perhaps more than any other place in this city of 33,000 people, the conditions in Mexico Chiquito illustrate the corrosive effects of an eviscerating economic recession that greatly slowed a formerly booming carpet industry. In one corner, a flimsy trailer doubles as a church and a rarely open doctor's office. A local doctor volunteers time once a month to help residents who cannot get to the hospital or who are afraid to go there. Before the promotoras came into Juan Cabrera's life, this sometime clinic was the only place he could go when he felt sick.

Cabrera has little hope of ever returning to do the low-wage work for which he originally left Mexico a decade ago. He and Estela are several months behind on rent. They keep a rising pile of medical bills in a shoebox.

"I really don't know where we'd be without their help," Cabrera says of the promotoras. Estela's eyes well with tears.

Translated literally, *promotoras de salud* means "promoters of health." But over the years these women and the program for which they work have become far more than that. They are also vital promoters of optimism, hope, dignity, and human connection. Started as a small health care advocacy project, these community-based lay health care workers provide a modicum of security for an immigrant community whose job opportunities have been dwindling in a tough economy and who've been pushed even further to the margins by Georgia's immigration policies. Immigrants here talk about the growing number of fathers leaving their families behind in search of work beyond this working-class city.

In 2011 Georgia's immigrants faced new challenges. That year, Georgia's legislators passed a law known as HB 87 that made it a crime to "harbor or transport undocumented immigrants" and makes it more difficult for businesses to hire people who do not have proper immigration documents. The law also gives local law enforcement officers authority to run immigration status checks on anyone arrested, detained, or pulled over even for minor traffic infractions. Whitfield County, of which Dalton is a part, is among the state's leaders in triggering deportation removals under Georgia's 287(g) program, which permits local police or sheriffs to use a controversial federal database to determine a detainee's immigration status. (In August 2012, a federal judge struck down the section of HB 87 that criminalized the "harbor and transportation" of undocumented residents. The U.S. Court of Appeals for the Eleventh Circuit upheld that ruling.)

Until the 1990s, Dalton, sitting in northwest Georgia near the Tennessee border, had not been a favored destination for Latino immigrants. But immigrants were lured here by relatively well-paying jobs in a then-booming carpet industry and also by work in chicken processing plants and seasonal agricultural jobs. In 1990, only 4 percent of Dalton's residents were Latino. By 2000, that share had increased to 40 percent, and by 2014, Latinos made up nearly half the city's population. In 2013, nearly 70 percent of students in Dalton's public schools were Latino and about 15 percent were still learning English. Immigrants make up 13 percent of Georgia's workforce, according to the Washington-based Immigration Policy Center. The Pew Hispanic Center, meanwhile, estimates that unauthorized immigrants make up 7 percent of the state's workforce, which is one of the largest shares of any state. Perhaps because immigrants settled in Dalton in such large numbers over such a short period of time, and in a place where people had little experience with Latino culture, the health care system had failed to adapt. Hospitals and clinics lacked Spanish-speaking interpreters. The notion of preventive health care, which would ideally include annual checkups, prenatal visits, and routine testing of symptoms as signals for underlying conditions, was unfamiliar to many newcomers who had either rarely consulted with doctors or made appointments only when extremely sick. Among all racial and ethnic groups, Latinos are the most likely to be without health insurance. About 40 percent of Latino immigrants and about a quarter of Latinos overall did not have health insurance in 2014, according to the Pew Research Center. Women in Dalton regularly went without mammograms and Pap smears. Men with chest pain never got checkups. People without proper immigration documents worried that merely going to a hospital would get them deported. Adults without English skills were forced to turn over control of their health care to their young children, who served as their interpreters.

But as more and more immigrants settled in Dalton, health care officials and advocates realized they needed to rethink traditional health care delivery models in which hospitals and doctors tended to wait for people to come to them. And so they looked far beyond northwest Georgia, and far beyond their own habits and protocols, to promote health and well-being in their changing community. The promotora program began not long after Nancy Kennedy, the executive director of the Northwest Georgia Healthcare Partnership, began to hear about successful promotora programs in Texas border communities. Health care providers, business leaders, educators, and local government started the partnership as an effort to improve community health. The nonprofit sits across the street from Dalton's one hospital and major clinics, making it convenient for promotoras, who often accompany patients to doctors' visits.

"We moved quickly to care management," Kennedy says. "We saw that once [patients] left the doctor's office there was a disconnect, and once we could go inside their homes we could understand the whys and hows and that was important."

In contrast to the punitive laws at the state level, the Promotoras de Salud program creates a supportive, protective community circle for immigrants, who make up a substantial share of the region's workforce. It connects Spanish speakers to a health care system that historically had not served them well and which, in many cases, immigrants simply did not trust.

The promotoras help the Cabreras and other immigrant families in myriad ways, all of them aimed at improving physical and mental health in the community at large and integrating immigrants into the health care system. Promotoras will deliver food from local pantries, accompany patients to doctors' appointments, and help people fill out medical paperwork. They are comforting, knowledgeable guides through the dizzying, often dehumanizing health care maze. In the Dalton area, the program's five promotoras de salud have served dozens of families in the trailer park where Cabrera lives with his family. In all, promotoras have 357 families on their caseloads. The women track each person's entry into and exit from the health care system. Until recently, records had been handwritten and kept in cabinets, but then a local software company donated a filing program, allowing the promotoras to enter the modern age and computerize their records. But Kennedy points out that because of limited funds and a small staff, the promotoras, no matter how hard they work, cannot possibly reach all the families who would benefit from access to health care and from their attention.

Foundation grants and local corporate support, including substantial dollars from the carpet mills that employ so many immigrants, sustain the promotora program. Promotoras are quick studies. They attend trainings and take advantage of health-related workshops at the hospital and other settings, so as to stay up on current knowledge. At the program's inception in Dalton, Kennedy and others recall, a lot of doctors and nurses resisted seeing promotoras as collaborators and partners, tending to view them instead as well-informed language interpreters. Some doctors and nurses did not seem to like the idea of having promotoras present at doctor's office visits. Now, Kennedy and others say, promotoras are increasingly the first professionals that doctors and nurses who work with immigrant patients will call.

When the program launched, the most pressing needs among immigrants included prenatal care and transportation, says America Gruner, the program's first promotora and first program director. Gruner left the program and founded the civic group Coalicion de Lideres Latinos (CLILA), Coalition of Latino Leaders.

"Pregnant women didn't know where to go, were not going to doctor's visits, and immigrants were also affected by transportation since the law stated they couldn't drive," Gruner says. "So many people wanted to get services and they couldn't, so we started to offer transportation." (As is true in all but eleven states, immigrants without authorization to be in the country are prohibited from getting driver's licenses in Georgia.)

"It was difficult at the beginning," Gruner says. "The doctors had to understand we were not there just to translate materials. We understood the people and we could educate them about health. It was intertwined."

For at least several decades promotoras de salud have been around in different incarnations in Mexico and other Latin American countries, specifically to bring health care and health education to the poor. In many cultures and nations, indigenous community members have long played important roles in providing health care and access to services and in acting as a bridge between established medical systems and often marginalized populations. Promotoras have grown more common in the United States since the 1950s. Under the Migrant Health Act of 1962 and the Economic Opportunity Act of 1964, the federal government mandated outreach to migrant worker camps and neighborhoods where people earned low incomes. As the Latino population grew in the 1990s, interest in the promotora model among doctors and health care officials in the United States also increased. Throughout the years, the roles of these lay health educators have remained largely the same—connecting people who historically do not have access to adequate health care or adequate information to keep themselves healthy. Keeping individuals healthy, of course, promotes and contributes to the health of the general population. Prevention and education reduce the number of costly visits to emergency rooms and the likelihood of emergency procedures. In that sense, the promotoras benefit not only their patients but the entire community as well.

Some days bring emotional challenges for the promotoras, whose involvement with and empathy for the local Latino community extends far beyond professional responsibilities. After a weekly wellness class on diabetes, the five promotoras learn that an eight-year-old girl they knew has just died of cancer. The tears flow. They console each other with hugs and gentle pats and then vow to keep it together for the rest of the day, which will include a visit to Juan Cabrera. The promotoras not only care for Dalton's burgeoning Latino population but also reflect it. Four of the five promotoras are Mexican. They've faced some of the same struggles that their patients have. Promotora Marisol Torres, who moved here from the Mexican state of Michoacán six years ago, is dating a young Latino man who complains of being targeted by authorities while he's driving. Another promotora, Cristina Valdovinos, is a single mother trying to teach her children how to navigate two cultures. Liz Casillas and Teresa Patterson are Mexican American. They both grew up in California facing their share of challenges fitting in and negotiating multicultural environments. Esther Familia-Cabrera, who is Puerto Rican, moved from the Bronx, New York, with her family to take the job as director of the Promotoras de Salud program. She's rarely behind her desk and is often visiting her own clients and accompanying her workers to their visits.

"You look at the promotoras and they *are* the community," Familia-Cabrera says. "It's important to have that when you are going out there to deal with some serious issues with families with little to eat, little to live on."

In their book *New Destinations: Mexican Immigration in the United States*, Víctor Zúñiga, of the University of Monterrey in Mexico, and Rubén Hernández-León, a professor of sociology at the University of California, Los Angeles, explore the causes and implications of Dalton's demographic transformation. Their work shows that immigrants, primarily from Mexico, trickled into Dalton in the 1980s and then came in much larger numbers in the 1990s as the carpet business kept growing. "That was an important magnet for some time," Hernández-León says. "During the golden years there were not enough hours in the day for them to work. Some worked at two carpet factories making a wage and things were good." The Mexican immigration transformed Dalton, he says, and also produced a generation of Mexican Daltonians who have adopted this small city as their own and do not intend to leave.

During the carpet industry's boom years, the Mexico Chiquito trailer park and the nearby Underwood Street area were Dalton's entry ports. People tended to settle there first and were able to save some money by working sixty or seventy hours a week. Then they moved out of the park and further up the road to a duplex. The workers and their families often integrated into the community through their jobs, through their church, or via involvement with their children's local public schools. Some managed to keep saving and to buy homes a few more blocks up. But then came the recession. The carpet industry's trouble was further compounded by unanticipated consumer trends. Not as many people wanted carpets in their homes, and consumers started choosing hardwood floors instead, Zúñiga explains.

Men had been predominant in the backbreaking carpet industry, where jobs usually paid above minimum wage. The downturn forced them to either switch to lower-paying service work or leave their families behind and take seasonal agricultural jobs outside Dalton and in some cases outside Georgia. As in other new immigrant gateways, Zúñiga explains, it was the educators in Dalton's public schools; priests and ministers in faith communities; and doctors, nurses, and social workers in hospitals who were among the first to hear from immigrants about the cultural barriers newcomers faced. Zúñiga and Hernández-León see programs like Promotoras de Salud as particularly constructive and effective means for integrating immigrants into the health care system and, in time, connecting them to the community at large. With more immigrants in Dalton and harsh laws being enacted, Promotoras de Salud has evolved into a kind of default human rights organization. America Gruner, the former Promotoras de Salud director, recalls a Latino man who had fallen from a tree and lapsed into a coma. Incorrectly assuming he was an undocumented immigrant, officials at a nearby hospital had wanted to pay his way to the Mexican border.

"He had a visa. He was legally here, but the [hospital's] social worker had no idea what a valid green card looked like," Gruner recalls. "We had to defend him, and that's why the promotoras are not only about health . . . it surrounds everything."

Gruner estimates that it took two years for trust to develop between the promotoras and other professionals in the medical field. She knew things had changed when an oncologist called the promotoras for help with a fifty-year-old man from Honduras with HIV and cancer who had not gone to his medical appointments in several months.

"That's when we knew that the doctors, community, hospitals understood the benefit," Gruner says.

Fidencio Vergara fully understands the benefit. "They are my family," he says in Spanish in the corridor at the Northwest Georgia Healthcare Partnership office. "They do so much. They speak up for me and they always listen to me."

Vergara, who is sixty-three years old and diabetic, is receiving chemotherapy treatments for colon cancer. His gait is labored and slow. Vergara arrived in Dalton eighteen years ago from Guanajuato, Mexico. He had been a machinist at nearby Beaulieu Carpet, but several years ago he lost that job and left the area in search of work. His declining health brought him back to Dalton and to the promotoras.

Vergara says his doctor often tells him he can't be released until a promotora de salud is there to pick him up and take him home. The promotoras see the doctor's insistence as an endorsement of their program and a sign of the growing trust people have in them. They are also happy to see Vergara participating in a diabetes education workshop held in a tidy conference room in the Northwest Georgia Health Partnership offices.

Before the workshop starts, one of the promotoras' colleagues calls from a cell phone on their way to the promotoras' office. The caller alerts the promotoras that police have set up roadblocks at several intersections. Some of the officers, the caller reports, are stopping vehicles and asking for identification. The promotoras now know that if attendance is light tonight, it means that people were probably scared away. About a dozen people sit around an oval table. The Latino community experiences high rates of obesity and diabetes and, the promotoras say, the nonprofit offers these educational workshops to try to reverse those trends. A plastic model of the human digestive system sits on the table. A healthy foods chart and some nutritious recipes get passed around.

"Together we can have a good life, with or without diabetes," Familia-Cabrera tells the group. "We'll help you get your medication. Don't cut the pills."

At the end of an educational lecture, a guest, Dr. Pablo Perez, finishes with a question that might seem off-topic. But it reveals a deep understanding of the priorities and concerns of Dalton's Latino immigrant community.

"Now who is happy with President Obama's move?" Perez was referring to the president's policy directive Deferred Action for Childhood Arrivals (DACA), which ended the threat of immediate deportation of younger undocumented immigrants who had been brought to the country by their parents. Many of the participants are parents or grandparents. They are all smiling widely back at Perez.

On their way out the door, several attendees stop to talk one-on-one with the promotoras. The promotoras remind people to take their diabetes medication, not to miss appointments, not to cut their pills in half, and to take full doses. Their message is that health matters and that the quality of a person's health will help determine the quality of a person's life. As important, though, the promotoras' mere presence sends the message that the immigrants who've settled in Dalton and helped it prosper are deserving, valued members of a community that cares for them during hard times.

MAINE

Lewiston
★

STAY CLOSE TO ALL THOSE THINGS

Children of the Somali Diaspora Find Their Way on Their Own Terms in America's (Formerly) Whitest State

In September 2012, the British Broadcasting Service (BBC) aired a three-and-a-half-minute mini-documentary about the concentrated Somali population in "America's whitest state," Maine. The film featured a nine-second interview with Robert MacDonald, the mayor of Lewiston, a quiet, inland old mill city.

Mayor MacDonald, well known among local reporters for uttering indelicacies that spawned viral news stories, was about to make his international television debut. On camera, the plump, white-haired MacDonald wore a bright yellow polo shirt and sat, hands clasped, on a wooden bench in the sun. He presented as relaxed and informal but spoke in a commanding tone.

Gesticulating and grimacing, the mayor spoke directly to refugees and immigrants: "You come here, you come and you accept our culture. And you leave your culture at the door."

After the BBC's reporters packed up and went home, Lewiston's Somali leaders and their supporters organized a rally to protest the mayor's remarks. A racially diverse group of residents started a petition calling for MacDonald's resignation. The beleaguered mayor granted a local TV interview to, he said, "clarify" his statements.

"I don't care," he told a reporter, if immigrants want to "celebrate" their "holidays . . . just don't try to insert your culture, which obviously isn't working, into ours, which does."

From the vantage point of Lewiston's Somali residents, the mayor's second interview had only made things worse. The media storm came fast, furious, and mostly from afar. The *Huffington Post*, NBC, Politico and Yahoo published critical stories. A few white supremacist bloggers, however, posted flattering commentaries.

Two years later, Lewiston High School's senior class president, Muna Mohamed, begins her second day of her eighteenth year on earth. She checks the time on her smartphone and exhales. She's glad to be a little early, to have no need to rush to her first-period class, Advanced Placement Biology. A loose bright blue dress falls to her ankles. A black hijab covers her hair and brushes her small shoulders. Amid her mostly bleary-eyed, shuffling peers, Muna's enlivening smile lights up her delicate features and, it seems, the hallways.

"Hey, Muna! Happy birthday," a boy with sandy-colored hair and baggy pants yells as he passes Muna in the cafeteria. "I meant to post a happy birthday [on Facebook] last night but I fell asleep!"

Muna laughs. "It's okay," she tells him. "Sleep is extremely important in the teen years!"

"Muna! OMG! Your birthday?" a svelte white girl in tight jeans says. "Happy happy!"

"Thank you. Thank you," Muna says.

Muna slips away from her admiring public and into class,

where she will take an exam on biology-related chemistry concepts. It is the second major test in this class already, and the term only just began a few weeks ago. In a friend's car heading to school that morning, Muna and a third friend, Kalgaal Issa, reviewed notes on organic phosphates, cellular respiration, and the differences between RNA and DNA.

After class, Muna and Kalgaal gather their books. Muna whispers to Kalgaal: "Did you think that was easy? I thought that was easy."

"Yup. No problem," Kalgaal concurs.

The coming months present more of a challenge. Like high school seniors everywhere, Muna has started stressing about researching colleges and about finding time to visit them, to fill out applications and financial aid forms. She's concerned about her test scores and essays and about fitting all this into her busy schedule. In addition to being senior class president and twelfth in her class of more than 350 students, Muna is also the student representative on the city school board. On top of that, she takes a class on school reform at Bates College. Registering for the ACT test on her mobile phone during a study period, Muna looks up at her classmates, perplexed.

"Um, why are they asking me on this questionnaire about whether this or that career interests me?" She looks up over her phone. "I don't know exactly what I want yet," she says, looking around at the friends gathered at a table. "I mean, do you guys know?"

None of them really know. The few girls who say they "kind of know" quickly agree that they definitely do not know whether they will still want to do in five years what they think they maybe want to do now.

This is what Muna knows: that she wants "to contribute something really concrete, really positive in society." And: "I don't see myself sitting at a desk where there is this computer and a phone and a fax machine and that's how you do your work." And: "Not a politician. Blah. No." And: "I can see myself out there talking with people, working with really diverse groups of people, raising awareness about racism or injustices and figuring out how to make things better." Or, maybe, she says, she would like to be a schoolteacher in a diverse school, or an adviser to "a really decent, good U.S. senator on education issues," or else "a Twitter activist" using 140 or fewer characters to "shine the spotlight on racism, sexism . . . all the isms." Or "maybe," she imagines, "an advocate for English language learners." The list of socially conscious maybes goes on for quite a while.

If Muna wanted to become part of the American main-stream, her brains, beauty, poise, and charm would surely allow her to make a seamless transition. But she and her group of academically successful, engaged, active Somali girlfriends purposely position themselves just outside that box. To some extent, they feel pushed out there by the assumptions and norms of the dominant culture, by people who judge or dismiss them for their hijabs, their faith, or their facial features. But for Muna and her friends, where they stand represents a conscious choice against the old brand of assimilation that Mayor MacDonald demanded.

"We kind of have to invent it," says Muna's friend Kalgaal. "It's not about following what someone else tells you to do."

"Yeah, and we are doing that," Muna says. "All of us are doing that. Sometimes it's hard. Wanting to be a part of things but also standing outside in your culture. For Somali girls it is maybe a little bit harder to just fit in, because for one thing, we wear clothing that is traditional to our culture and faith. We wear the hijab. And our parents do tend to protect us more. They don't like us out late, that kind of thing.

"It's different for boys," Muna adds, because "they have the choice of being perceived as 'African American,' so, in that sense, *American*. . . . We stand out more as distinct. And that can be hard. But I think it is a good thing because it gives you that strong foundation of knowing where you come from."

Muna, her friend Kalgaal, and the several other girls of Somali heritage who make up this civic-minded, scholarly circle don't have much to say about the mayor and his admonishments.

"Yeah, I remember something about it," Muna says. She rolls her eyes, shrugs her shoulders. "But all of us were busy with school stuff and whatever then." The mayor is old news.

Around Lewiston these days, it is extremely easy to find young people of Somali descent—often called the second or "1.5" generation—who are successful in all the varied, subjective ways one might define accomplishment: High grades. On track to college or professional career training. Class presidents. Drug and alcohol free. Physically fit, accomplished athletes. Lots of friends. Respectful of their parents and teachers. Civically involved. Happy. Caring. Critical thinkers. Personable. Many of the adults who counsel, teach, coach, and care about young Somali kids in Lewiston have watched these individual success stories unfold over the years and learned from them. They tend to agree that the most promising path toward success is one on which young people maintain strong ties to culture, native language, faith, and family while being accompanied by adults who encourage those connections.

"A lot of us, we began to figure out that the Somali kids you saw who maybe they are adjusting a little too fast, too much to the American teenage life, the partying, the rebelling against their parents? It does not turn out very well. At first maybe you might look at that and you think, 'Oh, that's great. Look how he's fitting in! He's got all these friends!' But you know, honestly, those were the kids who drifted, the kids we lost," says Lewiston High School's soccer coach, Mike McGraw, who also has taught biology for four decades. The majority of McGraw's players are of Somali descent or from other African nations.

"After seeing this kind of negative kind of assimilation happen over and over, I started telling the kids straight out. I'd say, 'Hey, hang on to your native language. Do not lose that. And keep your culture. And keep your faith. Listen to your parents. Stay close to your parents. Please stay close to all those things.'"

McGraw himself did what he calls "simple, human" things. In the first year with Somali kids on his team, he noticed that the white kids and the Somali kids changed into their game gear in separate areas of the playing field. McGraw literally forced the two groups to meet in the middle and don their gear together. He provided breaks and space for Muslim players to pray. During the Muslim holy period, Ramadan, when Muslim players fasted, "I made it clear that those team members needed support and encouragement and respect for doing something that was very hard."

In 2012, the American Psychological Association (APA) released a major report that came to more or less the same conclusion that Coach Mike McGraw had years before. The APA assessed "factors that impede or facilitate adjustment" for first- and second-generation immigrants and refugees and concluded that the large body of research on assimilation and what's called "acculturation," the process of adaptation to a culture different from one's home culture, "contradicts many of the assumptions in the popular culture." Mastering English and participating and engaging with American culture while remaining strongly identified with and participating in the home culture—researchers call this a "hyphenated" identity—seems to accrue the most benefits for young people. In fact, "overacculturation," a pulling away from or attempting to shed one's family culture in favor of the new culture, "may be harmful for immigrant children who pick up not only the new language but also negative cultural norms that are out of sync with their families," creating stress for both generations. Thus, the report recommends intentional "interventions" that enable language acquisition and opportunities for full participation in American culture and institutions while encouraging a strong "ethnic identity" that prevents those taxing clashes between parents and children.

★   ★   ★

Young Somali Americans like Muna and Kalgaal arrived in Lewiston as part of what city officials call "the migration," which made this down-at-the-heels former mill city of 35,000 people the "it" destination for Somali refugees. It all began around 2001, when city officials in this then nearly all-white community agreed to find homes for about ten Somali families. Officials in the seaside city Portland, a designated settlement site, had run out of affordable apartments and called on their counterparts in Lewiston to help. At the time, the residential vacancy rate in Lewiston was 20 percent versus just 3 percent in Portland, about forty minutes south. When the first Somali families got to Lewiston, church volunteers and city workers helped them settle into affordable apartments. Lewiston officials had previously settled a few dozen refugees from the small French-speaking West African nation Togo, a process deputy city administrator Phil Nadeau calls "unremarkable." This small success, Nadeau says, may have made federal officials confident about Lewiston's ability to assist refugees.

"But they of course had no clue what would happen," Nadeau says. "Nobody could have predicted."

Within weeks, Greyhound buses full of Somali refugees who had been previously settled in other communities in the United States began pulling into Lewiston's downtown station every day. At first families arrived mainly from the Atlanta, Georgia, metro area. (Muna's family, for example, relocated to Lewiston from Atlanta.) But as Nadeau and others later documented, by 2002 families were arriving, he says, from "almost everywhere"—a hundred cities in thirty-five states, including Indianapolis, Minneapolis, St. Louis, and Phoenix. By 2002, more than a thousand Somalis had arrived in Lewiston.

University of Maine sociologist Kimberly Huisman would later find that those first Somalis to be settled in Lewiston had begun calling relatives, fellow clan members, and friends in other parts of the United States to report that Lewiston had lots of cheap housing, quiet and safe streets, seemingly good public schools, and a small Somali community. A relatively generous welfare program and affordable health care were also draws. "Secondary migrants"—refugees settled in one place who later relocate—have helped establish concentrated Somali communities not just in Lewiston and Portland but also in suburban Minneapolis and a few other places. Lewiston's Somali community, though, is notable for its rapid growth and size. Lewiston's is quite likely the largest "secondary refugee migration" in the United States relative to a municipality's population, Nadeau says. Complicating matters in Lewiston is the fact that, unlike in officially designated refugee settlement sites, the federal government does not automatically provide money to mitigate the costs associated with assisting secondary migrants. Proving refugees' origins in order to get federal aid turned out to be a labor-intensive process that was not always successful. When refugees first arrive in the United States, they are placed with an official resettlement agency that has entered into a cooperative agreement with the U.S. State Department. (The agencies, such as Catholic Charities, usually have local affiliates across the country.) Those affiliates coordinate basic needs such as clothing, housing, and medical care for the first one to three months after a refugee's arrival. The federal Cash and Medical Assistance (CMA) program also reimburses primary settlement communities for up to 100 percent of certain services provided to refugees, including cash assistance and some types of medical care.

Meanwhile, in Lewiston, the buses kept arriving. As of 2014, city officials estimate that between 4,000 and 4,500 people of Somali descent now live in Lewiston. Educators report that about 30 percent of students enrolled in the city schools are black, the vast majority of Somali descent, though increasing numbers of students with origins in the east African nation Djibouti, Sudan, South Sudan, and the Democratic Republic of the Congo have enrolled in recent years.

★   ★   ★

A long, narrow eastern African nation with a 1,900-mile coast-line along the Indian Ocean and the Red Sea, Somalia has the world's largest share of refugees and internally displaced people. The vast majority of refugees being settled in Maine had made their way over Somalia's southern border to sprawling camps in Kenya, where they had lived typically for more than a decade, after fleeing one, several, or all these things: a brutal, full-scale civil war ongoing since 1991, an earlier civil war in the 1980s, total government collapse, thievery, torture, pillaging, loss of property and homes, destitution, rape, torture, violence, famine, and drought. Every year from 2008 to 2013, the Washington-based nonprofit Fund for Peace named Somalia the world's "most failed state" in its annual index. (In 2014, Somalia ranked second, behind South Sudan.) The U.S. Office of Refugee Resettlement reports that between 1983 and 2004, agencies resettled more than 55,000 Somalis in the United States.

"Most people, you know, the first thing they'd say is, 'Geez, aren't they all freezing cold?'" Lewiston's Nadeau recalls. The second most common question came with more of an edge: "Who authorized this?"

"Last time I checked, Lewiston, Maine, was part of the United States of America," Nadeau remembers responding more than a few times. "And in this country, people can move to wherever they choose."

The several thousand Somalis had indeed specifically chosen Lewiston, a place lots of others had left behind. For about a decade prior to the migration, more people were leaving Lewiston or dying than were moving in or being born there. But compared to Atlanta, Houston, and Phoenix, where Somali refugees had been corralled into large, crime-riddled housing projects, Lewiston presented as calm, quiet, and—most important—safe.

"I think Lewiston feels like a protective place to a lot of the Somali parents. I know that is true of mine," says Zahida Sheikh, a Lewiston High School senior, aspiring writer, and, with Kalgaal Issa, a member of the city's Youth Advisory Council. "Parents can really easily know where their kids are because there aren't a lot of places we young people can be."

And so it was that thousands of families, many with four, five, six, or more children, and sometimes grandparents, made Lewiston, Maine, their home. Most of the new residents had little to no formal education and no experience with the American workplace, and a large share of the adults were illiterate even in their native language, Somali.

The husks of several imperious mill buildings, with Italianate towers and mansard roofs, spread along the city's murky canal waters. The old mills offer daily reminders of a lost era when bustling, lively Lewiston anchored a regional economy bursting with jobs paying a living wage. Those days are long gone. In 2000—this is before large numbers of Somalis began arriving—nearly 60 percent of Lewiston's families with children younger than five lived in poverty.

Lewiston's new residents stood out. Most Somali women and girls wear, as Muna and her friends typically do, a hijab (head scarf) and, typically, a loose, long-sleeved dress that falls to their ankles. Some Somali men, usually from the upper classes, wear Western-style formal business attire or casual business clothes; others wear more traditional long tunics. Some men wear an embroidered cap called a koofiyad. Almost all Somalis are Sunni Muslims. Family is central to most Somalis, and their family size tends to be larger than is typical in the United States. Girls often have responsibilities for cleaning and cooking, and in some cases they provide much of the care for younger siblings. Economic life tends to be collective, with money pooled among relatives and close friends and sent back home to loved ones in Somalia or Kenya.

"The resentment and tension was palpable. And the level of misunderstanding about what Somali residents were getting in terms of assistance was pronounced," recalls Kim Wettlaufer, who coaches girls' track at the high school, owns a sandwich shop downtown, and is also executive director of the Trinity

Jubilee Center in Lewiston, which runs a food bank, offers daily meals to the hungry, and gives away donated clothing. Nadeau, the deputy city administrator, similarly recalls "crazy rumors" about "the city giving Somalis free cars, huge cash payments, refrigerators. It took a lot of effort to dispel these myths."

Fifteen years after the migration began, Wettlaufer says, "there is still an enormous amount of racism, but it's certainly not like it was. And part of what will improve things further is increasing the understanding of how much progress members of our Somali community have made. That is not to say there is not profound poverty still and there aren't challenges still. But what some of the young people have accomplished after not even a full generation here? It's stunning."

Somali-owned businesses—variety stores, clothing stores, and food shops—line more than half of Lisbon Street, which is usually busy with shoppers. An unembellished mosque sits next to Antonio's New York Deli and Bakery. A decade ago, Wettlaufer says, Lisbon Street (and downtown generally) "was a ghost town, lifeless and kind of depressing." Kennedy Park, behind city hall, bursts with the colors of traditional African clothing and the sounds of children playing. Somali mothers push strollers, hold their toddlers' hands, and socialize. On weekends, men, boys, and girls kick soccer balls around, littler kids chase each other, and families have picnics. At the Walmart in neighboring Auburn, African-born greeters, shelf stockers, and cashiers work alongside white employees.

Since the migration, Lewiston's crime rate has dropped, hitting a thirty-year low in 2010. The crime rate here is far lower than that found in other cities such as Portland and Bangor that have similar or higher shares of residents living below the poverty line. In 2011, researchers at the University of Maine published a book called *Somalis in Maine*. They found that Maine's relatively generous welfare benefits and access to free or low-cost health care were indeed important initial draws for Somalis but that those things became far less important over time. As the years went on, Somalis were more likely to list the quality of public schools, accessibility of nearby colleges, and safety as the most favorable features of life in Lewiston.

At one time it was absolutely true that a hugely disproportionate chunk of the city's general assistance welfare budget (half of which is reimbursed by the state) was spent on refugees. For example, in the 2001 fiscal year, about 53 percent of the budget went to noncitizens, most of them refugee Somalis. But by 2010, just 18 percent of that budget aided noncitizens, roughly reflecting the share of immigrants and refugees in the general population.

In 2013, Mayor MacDonald appointed Zam Zam Mohamud, a well-known and civically involved parent, to the school board. It was the first time an adult of Somali descent had served on the board. Mohamud's daughter, Hanan, a co-president of the Lewiston High School's 2009 senior class, had been the first student representative of Somali descent on the school board. Though Zam Zam Mohamud lost her seat in an election later that year, another Somali, Jama Mohamed, later won a seat on the board in a special election. Mohamed is communications director at the Lewiston-based Somali Bantu Youth Association of Maine, which provides English and citizenship classes and an array of youth programs.

In recent years, more and more students of Somali descent have been elected class officers at Lewiston High school, won statewide writing contests, experienced success on the girls and boys soccer and track teams, taken college-level classes at Bates College, won admission to highly selective colleges, and participated in the city's eleven-member Youth Advisory Council. In recent years, a young Somali fashion designer and 2014 Lewiston High School graduate named Sahro Hassan won local and national competitions for her small business, Uji Fashion, which produces clothing that is appropriately conservative for Muslim girls and women yet bold in its own way.

"What I remember are the teachers who liked that I was bringing my Somali culture and my faith into what I was doing," says Sahro, who studies fashion design at Mount Ida College, outside Boston. Two of Sahro's fashion shows, featuring her black and white friends as models, attracted local and regional media attention and dozens of supporters. Mayor Mac-Donald even showed up at one of Sahro's shows.

"You have to give credit to the Somali parents in these many cases of success because the commitment to education in the Somali culture is very strong and the challenges are not insubstantial," says Gus LeBlanc, Lewiston High School's principal from 2006 to 2013. From 1996 to 2006, LeBlanc was principal of Montello Elementary School, which also has a sizable Somali enrollment.

"The Somali migration was certainly the biggest and most unexpected challenge of my career," LeBlanc says. In the early days, he recalls, hardly any of the city's educators had much experience in creating and operating English as a Second Language classes. School officials had to "get out there" and find Somali interpreters so that school officials "could just have some basic understanding of what parents and kids were saying."

"We were ignorant, honestly," he says. "And I mean that not disparagingly but in the true sense of the word. We had to learn very, very fast. Not everyone did that and no way are things perfect."

Like LeBlanc, successful young people of Somali descent can easily list Lewiston's imperfections. But they prefer to focus on the people and interventions they just wish there were more of.

"Mr. McGraw and the kinds of things he'd say to us, this was very important. Maybe he believed it was a small thing . . . but no, it was a huge thing, the way he made sure everyone was bonded on that soccer team," says Khasin "Shobow" Saban, who graduated from Lewiston High School in 2011. "He made sure that the Muslim students had space to pray during the day and that when we were fasting during Ramadan, we were respected and supported." Around Lewiston, Shobow Saban is legendary, not just as a soccer phenomenon and former team co-captain but as a supremely gentle soul and stellar student. In May 2015 he graduated from Assumption College in Worcester with a degree in biology.

In 2012, when the mayor had issued his command that Somali residents "leave their culture at the door," a reporter had asked Shobow for his thoughts.

"I said that Somali people will never leave their culture at the door. We leave our shoes at the door!" He cracks up at his own joke. "Seriously, though, I can never leave my culture at the door. My culture is me. I am my culture," he says. Shobow is not comfortable speaking harshly about his fellow human beings. The most he will say about Mayor MacDonald is, "Perhaps one day he will learn that what he's suggesting causes great disaster for people. Without our culture, Somali people will float lost at sea in America."

Shobow plans on a career in health care, but his bond with the Somali community and his mother and five brothers will pull him home for a while. After graduation he will return to Lewiston to work at the Somali Bantu Youth Association of Maine (SBYAM), with the official title of "Youth Motivator." For several summers he had worked at the enrichment and social service organization, where he helped run a soccer clinic, took kids on field trips to the library, supervised noisy lunch periods, and got down on the worn carpet with little kids to play board games. On a recent visit back to Lewiston High School, some administrators suggested to Shobow that maybe he would like to teach biology at the high school someday.

"That is something I really would consider," Shobow says. "Lewiston is maybe not a perfect place. But . . . I saw the very good things that are possible between people who maybe you might think don't have anything to share. Somali, White, Muslim, Christian, whatever—we share something. We share that city. We live in that city together."

★   ★   ★

For two weeks during the past two summers Muna and Kal-gaal have taken a forty-minute bus ride west of Lewiston to the Seeds of Peace International Camp, deep in the woods of Otis-field, Maine. Emblazoned on the side of a small wooden build-ing, the words "The Way Life Could Be"—a play on the state motto "The Way Life Should Be"—greet visitors to the camp, which is set among tall pine trees on a calm, clear lake. Ebul-lient young people dressed in forest green camp shirts sit in cir-cles and talk intently. They cheer each other during camper-led announcements about interfaith prayer services, the upcoming play, and a cookout. They take canoes out on the water. Since 1993, Seeds of Peace has brought together young people on op-posite sides of global conflicts to get to know each other and, in the camp's words, meet their "enemies" face-to-face. Through dialogue and activities over two or three weeks, the program is designed to open young people's minds to what camp officials call "the possibility of a new reality."

In 2000, an educator named Tim Wilson, who was Maine's first-ever African American public school teacher back in the 1970s and has been director of programs at Seeds of Peace since it began, took note of the growing diversity in his adopted state—a change brought about mainly by the migration of So-malis and people from other African nations. He worked with local philanthropists and leaders to create the Maine Seeds pro-gram that year. Modeled after the well-established, recognized international program, Maine Seeds brings together a diverse group of teens from several communities, including Lewiston and Portland, to build relationships via its dialogue-based pro-gram, fight stereotypes, and then go back to their schools, where they identify problems and develop solutions to them. In recent years, the students have taken on a variety of challenges, includ-ing lowering social barriers between racial and ethnic groups, addressing bullying, expanding access to challenging school curricula, increasing support for students learning English, and raising awareness about drunk driving. "Seeds," as they call themselves, testify regularly at the statehouse in Augusta on a range of legislative matters, including English language learner policy, education funding, early childhood education access, and even raising the minimum wage.

Perhaps the best example of a local organization that offers myriad paths for participation in American culture and civic life, all purposely within a context of Somali and Muslim tradition, is the Somali Bantu Youth Association of Maine, where Shobow works and where he has been a board member. "Bantu," in this case, refers to a marginalized minority group in Somalia, members of whom began migrating to Lewiston from other parts of the United States in 2004. Mainly agriculturalists, Bantus, who tend to have a darker skin tone than ethnic Somalis, had a history of enslavement in Somalia and suffered discrimination for decades. Unprotected by traditional clan alliances, Bantus became particularly vulnerable during the civil war that began in 1991. Bandits and warlords stole food that Bantus had stored up, murdered Bantus, raped Bantu women, and destroyed their villages.

Shobow, along with SBYAM's founders, have Bantu roots. The distinction, relevant among older generations, is less relevant for Somali teens and children in the United States. SBYAM is open to all children, and Shobow says, "I am not even sure that a majority of the children here are Bantu. At this point, we've got kids from all over, Congolese kids, Somali, kids from Djibouti, Sudan. It does not matter."

SBYAM is situated within a community center that serves a heavily Somali Bantu neighborhood densely packed with dilapidated wood tenement apartments, many with satellite dishes mounted on sagging porches. After school lets out in the afternoon, the elevator up to SBYAM's second-floor headquarters is full of little girls in hijabs, arms hooked into backpacks, speaking a mix of English and Somali to each other, sharing chips or cookies. Boys, sweaty and short of breath, soccer balls wedged under their arms, squeeze together for the ride up. Kids saunter in and out to get homework help, to play games, to meet up with youth workers for soccer games, to just hang out.

A soft-spoken thirtysomething man named Rilwan Osman founded the nonprofit in 2008, with several Somali parents and leaders. "I saw that a lot of our youth, they were doing drugs and getting into trouble I think maybe because they were drifting from their culture and I would say, assimilating in a very unhealthy way," Osman says. "They were moving away from their parents culturally. The parents were losing control. The schools did not understand how to reach our kids. And there was no program. No one was dealing with this as a family issue."

Somali parents and other young Somali adults shared Osman's concern. Each week, they gathered in people's homes or at a mosque to talk and come up with a plan.

"We all agreed on the importance of education," Osman says. "In our culture, education is so valued, so important and we could draw on that."

To begin, Osman and others called around looking for space where Somali children could come in and either help each other with their school work or get help themselves The Lewiston Housing Authority, which oversees the Hillview apartment complex where many Somalis live, came through with a room to use. Kids also started coming to SBYAM's offices downtown for help, too. Soon afterward, the public schools started their own homework assistance and tutoring programs, allowing Osman and his collaborators to expand and diversify what they offered. Soccer had always been a beloved game in Somalia and a successful route of integration for Somali students in the United States—the perfect blend of Somali tradition and American pastime. So Osman and his colleagues created a youth soccer program after school, on weekends, and in summer for boys and girls. Hundreds of kids enrolled.

With small grants and donations and the support of dozens

of volunteers, SBYAM began offering English classes to parents and other adults. In 2009, Osman and his colleagues started a class that helped people fill out federal citizenship applications and prepared adult refugees and green card holders of many ethnicities to pass the three-part U.S. citizenship exam. To prepare for the citizenship interview, SBYAM volunteers role-play, taking on the manner and serious tone of a U.S. Citizenship and Immigration Services officer, asking things like "How many amendments does the Constitution have?" (twenty-seven) and "The House of Representatives has how many voting members?" (435). The citizenship test preparation class has helped more than a hundred Lewiston residents, most of them of Somali descent, pass the test and become U.S. citizens. (Refugees must apply for permanent residency the first year they are in the country, and they become eligible for citizenship only after living in the United States for five years.)

"Two-gen" is shorthand for a hot trend in human service programming that brings parents and young people together in a common institution to meet their needs simultaneously. But for Osman, who has always lived and worked within the family-centered Somali culture, assisting parents alongside their children came naturally. "You cannot do it any other way effectively in our community," Osman says. "When we have a meeting we tell the youth, 'Do not expect your mom to be like an American mom and do not expect your dad to be like an American dad.' And we tell the parents, 'Don't expect your child to be the way that they were back home or like you were back home.' They each need to come a little bit from where they are. Integration is important for success, absolutely. But it cannot be just the children we bring along. Both parent and child needs to see that this is a journey we are all taking together."

Lewiston is a curious place, with an endless supply of old and new stories about stumbling and standing back up, about intolerance and profound gestures of welcoming. Somalis were hardly the first newcomers to look at Lewiston and see new promise, to be able to imagine how good life could be there. And they weren't the first group to be feared, resented, and misunderstood.

Yankee industrialists from Massachusetts built Lewiston's mills. Irish, fleeing famine, began arriving in the late 1840s. They took jobs excavating canals and house foundations and built the Androscoggin and Kennebec Railroad lines. Irish women worked as maids and nannies for Yankee families.

"The arrival of numerous Irish in the 1850s created tensions and problems new to Lewiston," writes James Leamon in his book *Historic Lewiston: A Textile City in Transition*. "To many of Lewiston's Yankee inhabitants, the presence of the Irish did present a real threat, if not economic, then social and cultural. Not only did the Irish require and accept public welfare, but they also brought with them an alien religion and outlandish customs, not the least of which seemed to be an affinity for strong drink and petty crime." By the late 1860s, mill owners began recruiting French Canadians to work in the shoe and textile factories where business was brisk. "The French Canadians and others experienced discrimination and friction in relationships with the Irish and the Yankees," Leamon notes. Greek and Italians, in smaller but not insignificant numbers, followed the French. Older people in Lewiston knew of this history, at least vaguely. But by the time the Somalis showed up, most anyone who could have remembered the Irish nannies, the torched Catholic chapel, or the first French-speaking merchants was long dead.

Tensions had first bubbled up over the city's newest arrivals, the Somalis, in 2002. In October that year, Lewiston's then-mayor, Laurier Raymond Jr., appealed publicly to Somali elders and leaders, asking them to discourage their Somali family members and friends from relocating to Lewiston. In a letter published in the local paper, the *Sun Journal*, Raymond declared the city "maxed-out financially, physically and emotionally" after responding "valiantly" to the migration. As MacDonald's comments would a decade later, Mayor Raymond's letter attracted international media attention. An Illinois-based white supremacist group, World Church of the Creator, rushed to support the mayor and hold a rally to "unite the White people of Lewiston against the 'Somali invasion.'"

But once the white supremacists got to Maine, the few dozen people at their rally were eclipsed by a joyful throng of more than 4,500 people gathered at Bates College who had come out to support the Somali community. People had traveled from all over New England for the rally. Mayor Raymond, meanwhile, was on vacation—in Florida.

The big gathering had been organized by a group calling itself the Many and One Coalition. Formed hastily after the mayor's letter, Many and One brought together the local NAACP, the numerous religious communities in the region, social service providers, and local leaders. Maine's governor at the time, John Baldacci spoke at the rally. The state's two Republican senators, Olympia Snowe and Susan Collins, also attended.

Over the years, the reporters who came to Lewiston to write a version of the Somali story characterized Maine with ubiquitous shorthand: "the nation's whitest state." But in 2014, neighboring Vermont inherited the label of whitest state. By then, Maine had earned a new distinction: the "nation's oldest state." Its median age is forty-three, two years more than even Florida's and five years more than the national average. People from all ideological backgrounds can agree that this statistic is worrisome. The state needs to hold on to or attract far more young people at the start of their careers in order to have a tax base that can support retired or soon-to-be-retiring workers. Now it's young people like Muna, Shobow, Kalgaal, and Zahida that Lewiston needs more than ever.

In 2014, Muna was one of just two girls from Maine chosen for the prestigious, selective Girls Nation, a civic training program, sponsored by the American Legion Auxiliary, that brings top students to Washington, D.C., each summer. Muna met President Obama, which was "pretty cool," she says. "But what really stood out for me was that Maine was represented by two girls of color. Me and a Chinese American girl named Ellen. Funny, right? But I take that as a good sign."

There are signs of progress and, for young Somalis, constant reminders that the journey toward integration never ends. One year, at a public speaking competition in Philadelphia, Muna read an optimistic commencement address that Chris Gardiner, a once-homeless person who became a multimillionaire, had delivered at the University of California at Berkeley. She didn't advance to the final round. In written comments, the judge had praised Muna's "excellent speaking qualities" but questioned her choice of speech. He would have preferred, he said, for her to have read something "from the homeland" full of "pain and tears."

"I read that and I was like, huh?" Muna says. "I mean, seriously? My homeland? I am American. Maybe when you say the word 'American,' people don't see someone who looks like me. But I was born in Atlanta, Georgia. I live in Lewiston, Maine. Did he want me to say something very sad, about pain and tears, in my homeland of Maine?"

However, there is some pain in Maine, even for a girl like Muna, who makes it all look easy. "Just as one example," Muna says, after fifteen years lots of teachers still cannot pronounce even the most common of Somali names. "It's pretty disconcerting," she says, "when a teacher looks at the attendance sheet and says something like, 'Oh, wow! I'm not even going to try this one.' You know what? It's not funny."

Muna's close friend Zahida Sheikh is one of just a few students of Somali descent on the high school's yearbook committee. She enjoys the work. But it is also a setting where the school's dominant white culture is particularly salient. In a school where about 25 percent of students are not white, one student had complained (accurately) that only about 8 percent of the 2014 yearbook photos taken by yearbook staff featured students of color. For 2015, the club's faculty supervisor told students that the photos this year must reflect the racial diversity of the school.

Most of the teachers, Kalgaal says, "don't take advantage of the diversity in our school. Think about the perspectives our student body could add. Seriously? It could be amazing!" Kalgaal points out that even though roughly a quarter of the students at Lewiston High School are of African descent, "we don't even study South African apartheid in real depth or the Somali civil war."

"Or Asia," Muna interjects. "I mean, I'd really like to know more about Asia."

A week later, on Twitter, Muna writes: "School should be a place where students can have a conversation. Imagine how much we'd learn if we just sat down and listened to each other."

Soon after the decision not to indict white police officers who killed African Americans Michael Brown in Ferguson, Missouri, and Eric Garner in Staten Island, Muna, Kalgaal, and Zahida joined with fellow students putting up posters emblazoned with Garner's last words, "I can't breathe," and the final words uttered by other African American shooting victims, above the hashtag #blacklivesmatter. At first, school administrators ordered students to take the posters down. But after reporters from the *Portland Press Herald* paper ran a story about the "interrupted" protest, Muna, Kalgaal and other students met with administrators. The posters went back up. The school superintendent Bill Webster, even tweeted about it: "Approved #blacklivesmatter poster" with a picture of Muna, Zahida, and two friends standing in a high school hallway next to the posters.

Muna and Kalgaal's friend Margaruette Seguin, who is white, is a member of the city's Youth Advisory Council, along with Kalgaal and Zahida. (The Youth Council advises the City Council on youth-related issues and organizes community service projects.) Margaruette says she is grateful to Zahida, Muna, and Kalgaal for "deeply changing me, for making me see the world differently, for finally getting what white privilege means." Margaruette credits "going to a diverse high school" in general and Zahida's incisive tweets and her "insistence about calling out prejudice" in particular for "making me a better educated person in the world."

"I'm just glad you are my friend," Margaruette tells Muna over lunch one afternoon. "You know, for a ton of reasons. Not just cause of what you've taught me or whatever. It's so much more than that, obviously."

"Obviously," Muna says, smiling and tilting her head. "I know."

After college, Shobow will return home to Lewiston, at least for now. He's anxious to "help out my mother financially and be there for my brothers." And he is going to mull over the idea of teaching at Lewiston High School. "Being a role model for young people . . . wow," he says. "That would be something to cherish."

If the older generation wants to keep more young people like Shobow and Muna and her friends in Lewiston, Kim Wettlaufer of the Jubilee Center suggests that educators and counselors in the city "reexamine" an "educated American mind-set" that equates "progress with moving away physically and psychologically from one's parents."

"There is tremendous strength in Somali families," he says. "Close relationships, the communal way of life and the models of character and resilience are profoundly grounding. There is great honor in working within your community, staying close to your culture, being near as parents grow older, as you raise children. Why adhere to this idea that you need to break free from your parents and your community of origin? That way is not the only way. Who is to say it's the right way?"

The former Lewiston High School principal Gus LeBlanc

suggests that it's "long past time in Lewiston" for a "new way of talking" about refugees, immigrants, and the Somali community. This "new way," LeBlanc says, "would stop approaching the immigrant and refugee members of our community as problems to solve. I can understand why at first that was how it was seen. Look, we all made mistakes. I am sure I made my share of mistakes. But one thing we could do right now is try to bring back some of the Somali students to teach in our schools."

LeBlanc nods, in seeming agreement with himself.

"Yup. No doubt in my mind, that this would be one of the best things that could happen here, if the kids came back to us as our teachers."

A WAY FORWARD FOR A CHANGING NATION

Our success as a nation . . . is rooted in our ongoing commitment to welcoming and integrating newcomers into the fabric of our country. It is important that we develop a federal immigrant integration strategy that is innovative and competitive with those of other industrialized nations and supports mechanisms to ensure that our nation's diverse people are contributing to society to their fullest potential.

—*President Barack Obama, November 21, 2014*

The United States of America is, by far, the world's leader as a destination for immigrants. In 2013, the Census Bureau reported that a record 41.3 million immigrants—more than 13 percent of the population—lived in the United States. (Russia, ranking second, trails far behind, with 12.3 million foreign-born residents.) The United Nations reports that the United States is home to more than 19 percent of the world's immigrants.

Numerous experts and advocates have long argued that committing to immigrant integration is more urgent now than it has ever been. First and most obviously, the sheer size of the immigrant population alone should compel action. The Pew Research Center reports that from 1990 to 2012, the number of immigrants in the United States increased more than five times as much as the U.S.-born population (106 percent compared to 19 percent). In 2013, one in four children in the United States lived with at least one immigrant parent. Given immigrants' large numbers in our society, it follows that if immigrants do not prosper and advance, then the nation as a whole is less likely to prosper and advance.

Second, over the past two decades, immigrants have been settling in new areas of the country, particularly in the South, and in new types of communities, including suburbs and rural towns. Teachers, social workers, clergy, and government officials in such places tend to have little experience with immigrants from, say, Latin America, Asia, or Africa, whose experiences and cultures and native languages differ from those of the European immigrants who arrived in previous generations.

Third, during previous major migration waves, integration was achieved by what Michael Fix of the Migration Policy Institute (MPI) calls "mediating" institutions that no longer have a strong presence in our society. These included labor unions and political party machines that vied for immigrants' membership and provided guidance, social ties, and a sense of belonging in new communities.

Fix and his MPI colleagues point out that, unlike other nations such as Australia, some western European nations, and Canada, all of which also receive significant numbers of immigrants, the United States has no systematic policy for helping immigrants become self-sufficient, fully contributing members in their new society. Our federal immigration policy instead tends to focus mainly on the contentious matters of who will be let in, who gets to stay, and who needs to go. The federal gov-

ernment has no identifiable agency or office specifically concerned with integrating immigrants into the larger society.

"Integration of immigrants remains an afterthought in immigration policy discussions and remains one of the most overlooked issues in American governance," writes Fix. If it is
accomplished at all, integration is often achieved locally. It relies
upon public schools, faith institutions, decent men and women,
and cash-strapped nonprofits.

Though immigrant integration is typically championed by
progressive-minded organizations, the movement's foot soldiers
on the ground tend to be nonideological people with low profiles. This includes directors of English as a Second Language
centers, Chamber of Commerce members, mayors, city coun-
cilors, practical-minded bureaucrats, leaders of faith communities, and heads of nonprofits. Perhaps this is why the concept
and practice of immigrant integration have won support from
both liberal and conservative thinkers. Immigrant integration
proponents long ago crafted and stuck to a simple, factually
supported, nonideological message that stresses shared fate: the
health of our economy and of our democracy depends upon immigrants finding success, happiness, and commitment in their
communities and in the United States over the long term. In
other words, we depend on each other. If immigrants do not
find success here, neither will the nation as a whole.

That message seems to be sinking in. Opinion polls suggest
that Americans may support a proactive effort to bring immigrants more fully into the civic, economic, and social life of
the United States. A 2013 Gallup poll found that 88 percent
of adults favored providing undocumented immigrants with a
path to citizenship provided they pass a background check, learn
English, and pay a fee. The year before, 72 percent of Americans
agreed in a Gallup poll that immigration is a plus for the nation.

During my One Nation Indivisible journeys, I spent a lot of
time observing, interviewing, and sharing meals with people
from all over the nation and the world. Many of these men,

women, and teens were progressive-minded folks like me. We tended to think alike on most of the major issues of the day. But that wasn't true of all the people I met. I find it telling that it's the words from one conservative Republican state senator from Utah that came back to me most often during the writing of this book.

"Look, our state has changed," said Howard Stephenson, who spearheaded efforts to expand language education and other learning opportunities for his state's Spanish speakers. "The little rural communities, little towns are all changing. If you celebrate that, if you give our young people a place to blossom and grow and to really integrate, if you create the opportunity for all of us to integrate and to each come over to the other's perspective a little bit, how can that not be good for everyone?"

E Pluribus Unum

ACKNOWLEDGMENTS

I am most grateful to the dozens of people across the country who took the time to share their stories with us. Without you, there would be no book.

This book was made possible by generous financial support from the W.K. Kellogg Foundation and in particular our stellar program officer at Kellogg, Luz Benitez Delgado, who championed this project from start to finish. The Norflet Progress Fund also provided support for our stories on Mississippi, Utah, and Montgomery County, Maryland. Dolores Acevedo Garcia and her Diversity Data team at the Heller School for Social Policy have been important, steadfast supporters and collaborators along this journey. I have benefited from the work of many scholars, activists, and practitioners who helped me understand the field of immigrant integration, refugee resettlement, and the particulars of demographic trends: Manuel Pastor at the University of Southern California; Michael Fix and Margie McHugh at the Migration Policy Institute; Eva Millona of Massachusetts Immigrant and Refugee Advocacy Coalition; Westy Egmont at Boston College; Carola Suarez Orozco at New York University; Ahmed Samatar at Macalester College; Myron Orfield at the University of Minnesota's Institute for Metropolitan Opportunity; and Jessy Molina, David Lubell, and the entire staff of Welcoming America. I'm extremely grateful to my talented and insightful editor at the New Press, zakia henderson-brown. Great thanks as well to the entire New Press team and in particular to Sarah Fan, Marc Favreau, and Diane Wachtell.

I am grateful to so many friends and close colleagues. I feel incredibly lucky to have Fred Kimberk's presence and love in my life. Gina Chirichigno, One Nation Indivisible's co-director, was an invaluable contributor to this book in immeasurable ways and, more important, a dear forever friend. Kelly Garvin at the Houston Institute for Race and Justice, where One Nation Indivisible was based, provided editorial support and suggestions that greatly improved this manuscript. For more than a decade, Phil Tegeler, of the Poverty and Race Research Action Council, One Nation Indivisible's other home base, has long been a reliable, insightful, and supportive collaborator. In the final dark days of revision, Mark Kramer performed a heroic editing of the book's preface and reminded me why I write books like this. I am blessed to work with and teach remarkable students at the Harvard University Graduate School of Education. In the 2015 spring semester, the group I call "the People of A-118" reenergized me, expanded my thinking, and made me feel hopeful about the future of our country. You made this a better book—and made me a better thinker—in all kinds of ways.

Finally, to my spectacular sons, Will and Eli Kramer— THANK YOU for more than words and even ALL CAPS and even xoxoXXOOOoooxx could ever say. You are my most important achievements, my greatest joy. I love you to the moon and back.

ABOUT THE AUTHOR

Susan E. Eaton is Professor of Practice and Director of the Sillerman Center for the Advancement of Philanthropy at the Heller School for Social Policy and Management at Brandeis University. At Heller, she works with emerging and established philanthropists to inform social justice grant-making. Susan writes and lectures widely about immigration, racial inequality in education, racial, ethnic and economic segregation, and the practice of integration in the United States. She is the author of *The Children in Room E4: American Education on Trial* (Algonquin Books, 2007) and of *The Other Boston Busing Story* (Yale University Press, 2001) and is a co-author, with Gary Orfield, of *Dismantling Desegregation: The Quiet Reversal of* Brown v. Board of Education (The New Press, 1997). In 2011, she co-founded the storytelling project One Nation Indivisible, which gives voice to people creating and sustaining integrated schools and communities across the nation. Her writing has appeared in numerous scholarly and popular publications, including the *New York Times, Harvard Law and Policy Review,* and *The Nation.* She is also an adjunct lecturer at the Harvard University Graduate School of Education, where she teaches about the implications and opportunities of demographic change for public schools. She lives in Massachusetts with her two sons.

Publishing in the Public Interest

Thank you for reading this book published by The New Press. The New Press is a nonprofit, public interest publisher. New Press books and authors play a crucial role in sparking conversations about the key political and social issues of our day.

We hope you enjoyed this book and that you will stay in touch with The New Press. Here are a few ways to stay up to date with our books, events, and the issues we cover:

- Sign up at www.thenewpress.com/subscribe to receive updates on New Press authors and issues and to be notified about local events
- Like us on Facebook: www.facebook.com/newpressbooks
- Follow us on Twitter: www.twitter.com/thenewpress

Please consider buying New Press books for yourself; for friends and family; or to donate to schools, libraries, community centers, prison libraries, and other organizations involved with the issues our authors write about.

The New Press is a 501(c)(3) nonprofit organization. You can also support our work with a tax-deductible gift by visiting www.thenewpress.com/donate.